SKI SUNDAY

BBC TELEVISION'S PLANNED COVERAGE ON SKI SUNDAY 1983–84

Sun 4 December	Schladming	Men's downhill
Sun 11 December	Val d'Isère	Men's and Women's downhill
Sun 18 December	Val Gardena	Men's downhill
Sun 1 January	Garmisch-Partenkirchen	90m Jumping
Sun 8 January	Morzine	Men's downhill
	Pfronten	Women's downhill
Sun 15 January	Wengen	Men's downhill & slalom
Sun 22 January	Kitzbuehel	Men's downhill & slalom
Sun 29 January	Garmisch-Partenkirchen	Men's downhill & Super G
Sun 5 February	Cortina	Men's downhill
	Borovetz	Men's slalom & GS

Ski Sunday is on BBC2. *Grandstand* and *Sportsnight* on BBC1 will also cover the World Cup in their programmes. There will be complete coverage of the Winter Olympic Games on BBC1.

World Cup scoring:

	pts		pts		pts
1st	25	6th	10	11th	5
2nd	20	7th	9	12th	4
3rd	15	8th	8	13th	3
4th	12	9th	7	14th	2
5th	11	10th	6	15th	1

World Cup overall classification:

5 (women 4) best results – Downhill

5 (women 4) best results – Giant Slalom

5 (women 4) best results – Slalom

3 best results – Combined

World Cup individual titles:
5 best results

Order of departure:
In all disciplines the order of departure is based on the latest FIS points handicap list. The first group of 15 draw for departure. The rest follow according to list. A skier who has attained 90 points overall may start no. 16 if not already qualified for the first 15. If more than one has 90 points a draw decides numbers after 15.

Franz Klammer at St Anton

SKI SUNDAY
Olympic Year 1984

John Samuel

British Broadcasting Corporation

John Samuel has been covering the Winter Olympic Games and international skiing for The Guardian *since 1964, and has been Sports Editor since 1968. He is a keen skier himself and has written two books on the subject:* Love of Skiing *and* Ski-wise. *He has been the BBC's consultant on winter sports since 1968, and is the author of* Ski Sunday *and* Ski Sunday Supplement.

Nicholas Howe is staff correspondent with the US Women's ski team.

Published by the
British Broadcasting Corporation
35 Marylebone High Street
London W1M 4AA

ISBN 0 563 20221 1

First published 1983
© The British Broadcasting Corporation
and the Contributors 1983

Printed in England
by Jolly & Barber Ltd,
Rugby, Warwickshire

CONTENTS

Picture credits

Pages 3, 8 Daniel Rose; 10, 13, All Sport; 19 A.R.T. Foto; 21 Popperfoto (UPI/Tanjug); 23, 25 Colorsport; 27, 29 All Sport (Steve Powell); 30 Colorsport; 32 All Sport (Tony Duffy); 34 Colorsport; 42 BBC Hulton Picture Library; 44 Mansell Collection; 45 BBC Hulton Picture Library; 46, 47 Keystone; 49, 50 Popperfoto; 51, 52, 53 Keystone; 55 London Express News & Feature Service; 56 Keystone; 57 Colorsport; 59 All Sport (Tony Duffy); 61 Skate Magazine (Fred Dean); 62 Popperfoto (UPI/Ron Kuntz); 63 All Sport (Tony Duffy); 66, 69 Colorsport; 70 Daniel Rose; 71 All Sport; 72, 73 A.R.T. Foto; 74 Daniel Rose; 75 Key-Color, Zurich (G. Keller); 76 A.R.T. Foto; 77 All Sport (Robert Martin); 79 *top* Daniel Rose; 79 *bottom*, 80 All Sport (Tony Duffy, Robert Martin); 81 A.R.T. Foto; 82, 83 *left* R. Adlington Photo; 83 *right* John Samuel; 86, 87 Daniel Rose; 88 A.R.T. Foto; 89 Popperfoto (UPI/Pat Benic); 90 Daniel Rose; 92 A.R.T. Foto; 93 *top* Giuliano Bevilacqua, *bottom* Daniel Rose; 94 All Sport (Tony Duffy); 95 Daniel Rose; 96, 97, 98 A.R.T. Foto; 99 Giuliano Bevilacqua; 100 A.R.T. Foto; 101 Popperfoto (Pressens Bild); 103 Daniel Rose; 104, 105 A.R.T. Foto; 106, 107 Colorsport; 108 *top* A.R.T. Foto, *bottom* Colorsport; 109, 110 Colorsport; 111 Key-Color, Zurich (G. Keller); 112 A.R.T. Foto; 113 Colorsport; 114, 115 All Sport (Tony Duffy); 116, 117 A.R.T. Foto; 118 *top* Daniel Rose, *bottom* Key-Color, Zurich (G. Keller); 119 John Samuel; 120 A.R.T. Foto; 121 Popperfoto (UPI/Joan Eaton); 122, 123, 124 A.R.T. Foto; 141 Bild & News; 142 R. Adlington Photo; 143 Popperfoto (UPI); 144 *top* Popperfoto (UPI/Mike Ridewood), *bottom* Giuliano Bevilacqua; 145 Colorsport; 147 Popperfoto (UPI/Frank Leonhardt); 148 Daniel Rose; 149 *top* A.R.T. Foto, *bottom* Popperfoto (Bild & News/Mark Senn); 150 *top* Daniel Rose, *bottom* A.R.T. Foto; 151 Popperfoto (Bild & News/A. Mettler); 152 Popperfoto (Bild & News/Bazzuri); 153 Popperfoto (UPI/Pat Benic); 157 *left* & *right* Popperfoto, *centre* Keystone; 158 *left* Keystone, *right* Key-Color; 160 *left* Popperfoto (UPI/Photopress), *right* Colorsport.

Biographies

ALL SPORT: 126 Buergler (Don Morley), 129 P. Mahre (Steve Powell), 137 Nelson, Moesenlechner (Tony Duffy); A.R.T. FOTO: 126 Erlacher, 127 Giorgi, Girardelli, 128 Kerschbaumer, Krizaj, 129 Mader, Lee, 130 Pfaffenbichler, Raeber, 131 Sbardellotto, 132 Toetsch, 133 Attia, 136 Kirchler, Magoni, Merle, 137 Maricich, Quario, 138 Serrat, 139 Waldmeier; KONRAD BARTELSKI: 126 Enn, 130 Mueller, Orlainsky, 132 A. Wenzel, 139 Walliser, H. Wenzel; GIULIANO BEVILACQUA: 131 Stenmark; BILD & NEWS: 125 Brooker, 127 Gruber, Heinzer, 128 Hoeflehner, Kernen, 129 Luethy, 131 Resch, 133 Ehrat, 134 Figini, 135 Graham, Haas, 136 Lehodey, 138 D. Tlalka, 139 P. Wenzel, Winkler; BLIZZARD SKI: 128 Klammer; BONGARTS: 139 Wiesler; BULGARISCHER SKIVERBAND: 130 Popangelov; CANADIAN SKI ASSOCIATION: 135 Haight, 138 Sorensen; NIGEL CHAPMAN: 133 Cooper; COLORSPORT: 126 Edalini, 127 Heidegger, 131 Strand, 132 Vion, 135 Kinshofer, 136 McKinney, 137 Oak; JUTTA FAUSEL: 129 Mair; JUGOSLAWISCHER SKIVERBAND: 125 Benedik, 127 Franko; KEY-COLOR, ZURICH: 125 Buergler, 126 de Chiesa, 128 Julen, 130 Podborski, 133 Barbier, Chaud, 134 Gerg, 136 Konzett, 137 Oertli, 138 Rey; KEYSTONE, ZURICH: 126 Cathomen, 130 Meli, 131 Stock (Votavafoto), 132 Wirnsberger (Votavafoto), Zurbriggen, 135 M. Hess, 138 M. Tlalka; SAMMY MINKOFF: 138 Steiner; POPPERFOTO: 125 Andreev (NTB/UPI), 126 Fjaellberg (Pressensbild), 127 Frommelt (UPI/Heirler), 129 S. Mahre (UPI/Heirler), 131 Strel (UPI/Bild & News), 132 Weirather (UPI/Heirler), 133 Eder (UPI), 134 I. Epple, Flanders (UPI/Sanden), 135 E. Hess (UPI/Mellace), 136 Kronbichler (UPI), 137 Pelen (UPI/Mellace), 140 Zini (Erwin Wyrsch); PETER POSPISIL: 133 Charvatova, 134 Soltysova; PRESSE-SPORTS: 134 Emonet, 138 Quittet; DANIEL ROSE: 126 Canac, 127 Gaspoz, 131 Strolz, 134 M. Epple, 135 Gros-Gaudenier, 137 Preuss; TANJUG PHOTO (UPI): 140 Zavadlav; US SKI TEAM: 128 Johnson, 133 Armstrong (Powers Photos); VG-FOTO: 134 Fjeldstad; VOTAVAFOTO: 131 Stoelzl, 135 Gutensohn, 139 Vitzthum.

Maps and diagrams by Line and Line.

FOREWORD

David Vine

On 17 December 1947, a BBC Television programme 'Picture Page' included a short interview with a Group Captain Collins and seven members of the RAF Bobsleigh Team. Two months later, the same programme squeezed in another interview with Mr J. Crammond, the British Cresta Run champion. Those are the facts you will find in the BBC archives under the heading of 'Winter Olympic Games coverage, St Moritz, 1948'. That was it! And if you turn the pages and thumb through another four years to 1952, you won't find much more under the 'Games' heading. For 1952, Oslo in Norway, there was no coverage at all except for two 'bought-in commercial films' transmitted the following year, one on skiing and one on skating. In other words, snow sport was 'something that happened abroad' which was of little interest to the inhabitants of Bolton, Basingstoke and Bournemouth. My goodness, how it's changed!

Four years ago, the lights were still burning in homes throughout Great Britain as BBC Television transmitted from Lake Placid, USA, at 3.45 *in the morning* and four and a half million people were fascinated by the brilliance of a certain Mr Robin Cousins. Previously, at a more civilised viewing time, millions more had shared the thrills of downhill ski racing. From Alpine to Bobsleigh, from Biathlon to Skating, Jumping and the other ingredients of the snow and ice carnival, the Winter Games are now one of television's 'banker' events in a calendar crowded with rival attractions – a far cry even from the days of 1956 and the VIIth Games in Italy, the first to be televised live. For the BBC, Peter Dimmock and Max Robertson made the trip, accompanied by one producer. One entry in an official ledger mentions '11 reports, overall cost £725'. (Let it be quickly mentioned that only a small proportion of that found its way into the pockets of the personalities behind the microphones describing the string of successes by the Russians and the grand slam Alpine runs of Toni Sailer, the legendary Austrian!)

And now it's Yugoslavia and venues in Sarajevo – like Mount Bjelasnica – which have had us all exercising our tongues since the *Ski Sunday* Alpine team's visit for the World Cup races there last winter. It is always the proud boast of

Nothing to take away the moment of unashamed and honest emotion of racer, spectator, television viewer – and commentator: David Vine interviews Peter Luescher, loser into winner at St Anton

every organising committee that 'these Games will be different'. After my visit there, I can believe that. Where else has anyone seen the world's finest downhillers start their run from the third floor of a restaurant, built on the top of the mountain to give it the extra few metres in height and length required by the rules? Oh, yes, they do – and to be fair it works, with what should be fascinating pictures as they launch themselves down a chute like ski jumpers, hopefully having remembered to leave the coffee cup behind! Since the World Cup races there, when the much talked about 'guaranteed snow' had mysteriously turned to mud and slush, the controversial staircase course, a succession of bone-jarring jumps, has undergone a few changes. It would be unfair to prejudge the Olympic Games on the evidence of last winter and there was ample evidence to show that Mount Bjelawhatsit can provide us with an Olympic spectacle. The surrounding scenery is spectacular and with BBC Television planning forty hours and more of programmes – a big increase on Lake Placid four years ago – the 1984 Olympic champions are certain to become even more well known and talked about than their predecessors.

And who will they be? The winter months of the World Cup leading up to the Games will provide the better clues and pointers in a season where I think we'll see more changes on the success and failure sheets than we have in the last ten years. The Austrian and Swiss domination of the mountains is already a thing of the past, with Canada and the United States having produced the Podborskis, the Brookers, the Mahres and a clutch of others. It is no secret that their European rivals have become a little red-faced with tremendous pressure being exerted on the ski coaches, trainers and administrators to ensure that the millions who watch live ski-racing either on the mountainside or on their television screens in the towns and villages surrounding the resorts are cheering 'home successes'. It is no longer just a question of pride. Television and the publicity it generates has made success on the slopes by a racer risking all every hundredth of a second a significant entry in the profit and loss accounts of the commercial companies involved in a multimillion-dollar industry.

But nothing can take away that moment of unashamed and honest emotion of racer, spectator, television viewer – and commentator – when the time clock shows that, somehow, that fraction of a second has been carved from the time of the previous leader and, barring another miraculous run by an unheralded and virtually unknown name on the list of those still to come, the gold is won. I include the commentator in that list above without hesitation, and if you were able to stand behind the rows of us tucked into our telephone-box cubicles as the race progresses, you would understand why. If you were not able to see which racer was on the hill, you could tell by the pitch of the voice coming out of the appropriate booth – especially if it's an Italian. Three months or so on the circuit, living with the racers and the back-up teams, sharing the champagne one night and sharing the hours of video watching the next when it's all gone wrong, almost has you convinced that you can feel the bruises. One of my Continental colleagues is not only convinced – he went one better. As his country's no. 1 racer suddenly 'got it all wrong' and flew like a weather-beaten sparrow through the air, he leaped to his feet, forgetting the size of the commentary box he was working in. Forehead hits window catch, gash appears on forehead, and with blood dripping on to his record cards, he just manages to catch a glimpse of his racer – walking away from the scene of the disaster, unmarked. The commentator spent the night in bed and in bandages. The racer sent him up a drink from the hotel bar. This skiing business will always get you in the end . . . or somewhere.

Bjelasnica – White Mountain – men's downhill site starting on a restaurant roof (below) which pitches the racer straight into a 51° chute

1

THE WELCOME IN THE RED SNOW

In the last six hundred years Sarajevo has been host to sultans, kaisers, führers and commissars. From 8 to 19 February 1984, it welcomes the XIVth Winter Olympic Games, and an altogether friendlier occasion it should turn out to be than some of the previous invasions it has suffered. All the same, the 1,700 athletes from 46 countries, 1,000 officials, 5,500 media people and 25,000 visitors will much exercise the resources of the first Communist country to stage a Winter Games, a festival with built-in geographical tripwires.

Most of Yugoslavia is mountainous. From the Alps of Slovenia in the north-west down the Dinaric Alpine spine to Bosnia and Herzegovina – the central republic hosting the Games – on to Macedonia, Serbia and Basnia in the south, Yugoslavia is rolling sierra. Little of it is high mountain, even in the far north near the Austrian border. Around Sarajevo, a city of 450,000 inhabitants, the mountains are between 4,000 and 5,000 feet, though Bjelasnica (Bjel-ASH-nee-tza) – the White Mountain – fifteen miles out, rises aggressively, domelike above the rest.

At 6,780 feet this is the men's mountain. The downhill starts on its restaurant roof, plunges down a 51° chute under a balcony that provides the idler with spectacular views of the province, then ejects the racer over 700 feet of bare, windswept switchback before the trees and bumps swallow him. The downhill course is one of the major facilities Sarajevo is acquiring for itself in a £90 million operation which leaves many Yugoslavs incredulous, for this is a country with a $20 billion foreign debt and 30 per cent annual inflation. Its per capita income is $2,500, which is among the lowest in Europe, yet much richer countries – Japan and Sweden – were beaten in the IOC voting at Athens in 1978 to decide the host in 1984.

The XIVth Games offer Yugoslavia a major opportunity to assert its place as a winter sports centre. The city of Sarajevo cannot in any real sense be regarded as a ski resort. It is the capital and seat of government of Bosnia and Herzegovina, one of Yugoslavia's six republics, and the hub of a region which boasts up to two metres of snow. Hard by the downhill start, Bjelasnica has boasted a meteorological station since 1892, such is the confluence of weather when warm, moist Mediterranean winds lift up to meet the chills of Continental highs. The 1983 competitions were hit by wildly varying weather which the organisers desperately hope to avoid in 1984. A former partisan, now on the organising committee, looking over the miserably bare slopes of Bjelasnica, said it was the worst snow for fifty years. 'It would have been bad for us in the war . . .' And he made a throat-cutting gesture.

The idea to host a Winter Games was born in the mid 1970s at a mountain lodge overlooking Sarajevo. The Yugoslav president, Tito, a keen hunter and sport enthusiast, enjoying a fireside chat with Bosnia political leaders, was taken by the idea and things happened quickly after that. He died, aged eighty-eight, in 1980, but preparations for the Games went ahead. Slovenian leaders argued that their long tradition of winter sports and access to central Europe made them a better centre to house and feed visitors, but the Bosnians retorted that the Games offered them a chance to develop a relatively deprived region and turn its beautiful and largely unknown mountain areas into a worldwide attraction.

Many problems have had to be faced. Sarajevo, industrial and frequently fog-bound, needed a spur to clean itself up and capitalise on its history. The Turkish conquest of 1435 left it second only to Istanbul as 'the most beautiful city in European Turkey'. The mosques, clock towers, bridges and narrow alleys of the old town give it considerable atmosphere, but clean-air and major drainage works were necessary to remove the Dickensian grime. To older generations and students of history, Sarajevo has a grim past. A frontier town of the Austro-Hungarian empire, it witnessed in 1914 the shooting by Gavrilo Princip, a 19-year-old Bosnian student, of the heir to the Austro-Hungarian throne, Archduke Francis Ferdinand, and his morganatic wife Sophie. The two shots set off a chain of events which were to engage major European countries in a war which killed or maimed twenty million. Princip's memory is honoured with a museum and his footmarks cast in concrete, for Yugoslavia did indeed find independence subsequently. Now, on nearby placards, the world is invited to the XIVth Winter Games in a spirit of peace and understanding.

Funding problems are largely solved by television and marketing revenues of just over a hundred million dollars. It is estimated that 2.5 billion people will watch the Games on television, and Communist minds have grappled with everyone from the Coca-Cola Company of Atlanta to Ooh La La Inc. of Monterey Park, California, for sponsorships and licences to meet the bills. Vucko, or 'Little Wolf', is the Games mascot, and his cheerfulness is manifest in Sarajevo's determination to make things work in spite of its meandering history and lack of major winter-sport expertise.

Some $45 million has been raised by the Yugoslavs themselves, the sum equally divided between the city of Sarajevo, the Bosnian Republic and the Yugoslav Federation. Individuals and industrial groups have contributed a percentage of

Trebevic bob run, a joint course with the luge

earnings for five years, and there has been massive public support in spite of costs. A new network of roads has been created to service the satellite centres up to twenty miles from the city centre. A new hotel has been built to house the IOC and international sports federation members and officials, but private homes will be used to augment the city's twenty-five restaurants and fifteen hotels. Two complete housing settlements were being built at a frantic rate in 1983, one as a village for the athletes and the other for the press, both westwards of the city centre, following the course of the rambling river Miljacka. Food is cheap, with the Central European stand-bys of veal, pork and chicken augmented by Greek and Turkish moussaka and kebab, and with wine abundant and generally good. Yugoslavs are inclined to toast their guests with the word 'Zivili' (Zhee-vu-li) while dashing down a slivovitz (plum brandy) of paint-stripping quality. It is a hospitality to be sampled with caution.

The city is especially proud of its brand-new figure- and ice-skating stadium known as the Zetra, costing $18.5 million and completed just in time for the World junior figure skating championships before Christmas 1982. Its costs per square metre were less than for a town house, partly because the shell has been left unlined so that pipes weave and curl like intestines. Immediately adjacent, the outdoor speed-skating oval attracts huge numbers of young city dwellers, the

Bjelasnica – Men's courses

	Downhill	Giant Slalom	Slalom
Start	2,076 m	1,745 m	1,572 m
Finish	1,273 m	1,363 m	1,363 m
Vertical drop	803 m	382 m	209 m
Length	2,994 m	1,122 m	553 m
Average gradient	28%	36%	40%
Maximum gradient	60%	60%	60%
Minimum gradient	5%	6%	22%

whole augmenting the existing sports complex, the Skenderija, which includes an auxiliary indoor skating rink and, for the Olympics, the Press Centre.

Bjelasnica stages the men's giant slalom and special slalom, as well as the downhill, and on a high plain forming one of its shoulders, known as the Plain of Igman, are the Nordic trails, set off at one point by the twin 90- and 70-metre jumps. The trail area, landscaped into the firs, is known as Veliko Polje (Big Field) and the jump stadium as Malo Polje (Little Field). At Trebevic, on a terrace above the old town connected by road and cable car, Sarajevo has built a combined bob and luge run for £4 million. The designer, Gorazd Bucar, a city engineer, has tried to answer the criticisms of both bobbers – that a luge run is too tightly curved – and lugers – that a bob run is too widely curved. He has also done it in sections so that everyone from beginner to expert can have a go. Like a necklace in the dark, it is Sarajevo's most wondrous new toy.

Jahorina, an existing facility twenty miles to the east of Sarajevo, hosts the women's downhill, giant and special slaloms. The height of the top station is 6,275 feet and the slopes are served by five chair and five drag lifts. Pale, a community of about 14,000, ten miles out of Sarajevo, services the mountain, which is another ten miles away. There is one hotel on site, the Jahorina, with 416 beds, the nearest Sarajevo comes to a resort facility. Few of the women World Cup downhillers in 1983 thought the downhill course much of a challenge, though the snow was as poor as for the men who had to cope with Bjelasnica's bumps and flat landings. Jahorina is a relatively flat course with a narrow, steep gully in the middle which has to be set more like a giant slalom. It is likely to suit the technically superior racers.

It will be a surprise, though, if Sarajevo proves a technical occasion in many other senses. At Sarajevo airport in February 1983 there was no taxi with a ski rack. There weren't too many planes, either, because of the fog. The airport is

Jahorina – Women's courses

	Downhill	Giant Slalom	Slalom
Start	1,872m	1,665 m	1,840 m
Finish	1,326 m	1,328m	1,629m
Vertical drop	546m	337 m	211m
Length	2,041 m	1,332 m	511m
Average gradient	29%	28%	35%
Maximum gradient	56%	50%	49%
Minimum gradient	9%	12%	9%

being provided with up-to-date aids. And there is always Mostar, nearer the Dalmatian coast, which has less fog though it is five hours away by road. Sarajevo will have its answers, like the taxis roaring around with skis winkle-picking from their rear windows and boots. You will just have to know when to duck.

2

A GUIDE TO ALL THE EVENTS
The Medal Prospects 1984

Alpine Skiing

Bjelasnica
Men
9 February/*Downhill*
15 February/*Giant Slalom*
19 February/*Special Slalom*

Jahorina
Women
11 February/*Downhill*
14 February/*Giant Slalom*
17 February/*Special Slalom*

There are three Alpine events for men and women in the Olympics – downhill, special slalom and giant slalom – all run according to the conventional rules of the International Ski Federation (FIS), but with no more than four skiers (and the reigning champion) entering from each country. The Alpine combined, consisting of downhill and slalom, was included in 1936 and 1948, but since 1952 medals have only been awarded for the three specialist disciplines. In 1936 medals were given only for the combined, and in 1948 for the downhill and special slalom and also the combined. Giant slalom was introduced at Oslo in 1952.

In all three events, skiers race individually against the clock. The top fifteen, according to the FIS standings, are drawn to get the best snow after not less than three forerunners, or *vorläufers*, have made a fair track and tested the organisation. Downhillers must have a minimum of three training runs on the competition course, and in extraordinary conditions, for example heavy snow, at least six skiers from the back of the field may run before the no. 1. Downhill has only one run. After the top fifteen have gone down, skiers race according to their place in the FIS rankings. In special and giant slaloms there are two runs on different courses with combined times determining placings. The starting order for the second run is according to the finishing places in the first run, except for those in the first five places, who start in reverse order – fifth starts first, fourth second and so on down to first, who starts fifth.

Where the downhill is primarily a test of speed, courage and fitness, the slaloms test technical skills including various types of turns and, in the case of the longer, hybrid giant slalom, speed in traverses. Slalom competitors are not permitted to test their courses, but they may inspect them from the side within one hour of the start. The memorising of the course is an important part of the challenge.

In all three disciplines skiers must pass between manned control gates formed by a pair of poles, these days usually plastic and hinged at the bottom to reduce injury risk. They are beflagged in specific colours to aid course identification, particularly in poor visibility. Because of the high speeds of modern downhill – an average 60 mph with top speeds approaching 90 – delays because of blizzard, bad light, rain or gusting wind are more frequent. Both feet must pass through the gate, but a skier can finish on one ski. If any gate is missed a skier is disqualified unless he climbs back and skis through the missed gate. Gatekeepers deliver a record of disqualifications to the referee after the first run of a slalom, and offending racers are not allowed a second run. All Olympic slalom runs are videoed.

Racers can be given a re-run if an official errs or there is unfair intervention by a spectator or animal. Provisional re-runs are permissible while awaiting firm evidence. A skier can be disqualified for being late at the start, receiving assistance, failing to wear his official start number or altering it, or disturbing another competitor on his run.

An Olympic or World Championship downhill must not be less than two minutes for men and 1:40 seconds for women, which effectively means between two and three miles for men and one and a half miles for women. The vertical drop should be 800 to 1,000 metres (2,624 to 3,280 ft) for men and 500 to 700 metres (1,542 to 2,296 ft) for women. Gates must be eight metres wide or more, and the course at least 30 metres wide in its faster sections. Slopes average 30° to 35° but some gradients will be as much as 50°.

The special slalomer must weave through a maximum of 75 gates for men and 60 for women, with vertical drops respectively of 180 to 220 metres (590 to 720 ft) and 130 to 180 metres (425 to 590 ft). Since at least a quarter of the course must exceed 30°, the average length for men is about 550 metres, or a third of a mile, and for women 460 metres. A slalom gate is between four and five metres (13 ft and 16 ft 3 in) wide. The gates are of four main types – open (across the face of the slope), closed (straight down it), vertical combination, and hairpin.

Giant slalom has a length of about 1,300 metres (four-fifths of a mile) and a vertical drop of 300 to 400 metres (925 to 1,312 ft) for men and 300 to 350 metres (925 to 1,150 ft) for women. The number of gates must equal 15 per cent of the vertical drop plus or minus five gates. Turns in GS are made higher and faster through the gates than in special.

World Championship medals have hitherto been awarded in addition to Olympic medals, but the FIS at its Sydney Congress in 1983 decided to increase the frequency of their own championships and to discontinue awarding medals on Olympic occasions. Instead of one world championship in the even year between Olympics, the 'worlds' will now be held in each odd year. Thus, between Sarajevo in 1984 and Calgary in 1988, FIS will stage Alpine world championships at Valtellina (Italy) in 1985 and Crans-Montana (Switzerland) in 1987. Nordic 'worlds' will be held at Seefeld (Austria) in 1985 and Oberstdorf (West Germany) in 1987.

FIS in 1982–3 approved Super Giant Slalom, a longer, one-run giant slalom, for World Cup, and at their 1983 Sydney Congress agreed it should continue in 1983–4. A separate points classification will be introduced in 1984–5, answering criticism of specialists in the shorter, two-run giant slalom that the Super was primarily intended to encourage downhillers out of their specialism and that they should not be penalised by taking aboard a substantially different discipline. Super G is not included in the 1984 Olympics but experiments will continue with a view to its inclusion in world championships and the 1988 Winter Olympics.

Congress at the same time abandoned the 'B' licence system whereby skiers – notably Ingemar Stenmark – effectively skied as professionals, making their own terms with equipment manufacturers. Now there is only one category of skier. National Federations may pay 'broken time' – reimbursement for money they might have been paid in other jobs – and provide trust funds for retirement or premature finish to a ski career. Existing 'B' licence skiers were given the right to continue their personal arrangements until retirement. Stenmark subsequently entered into a lengthy battle to regain the right to compete in Sarajevo.

Four FIS points lists governing individual start places were decided upon. That on 1 November 1983 took account of performances up to 1 October. Other lists will be published on 5 January 1984 (performance deadline 27 December 1983), 3 February (for 30 January), and 27 April (16 April). World Cup events must start by 10 am in December and January and 9.30 in February and March.

At Sarajevo, assuming even the challenge of Stenmark, slalom and giant slalom gold medallist at Lake Placid, Phil Mahre must be favourite to gain his first Olympic gold in either or both of the slaloms. He missed out in the world championships at Schladming in 1982, where his brother Steve won the giant slalom and Stenmark the special, so Sarajevo will be a special target. Bojan Krizaj, on home snow, may find the pressures heavy in the special slalom, but he won Markstein in 1983. Steve Mahre, Stig Strand, Marc Girardelli and Andreas Wenzel, the silver medallist at Lake Placid, are others who know how to win in the most open of men's competitions. Two Swiss newcomers, Max Julen and Pirmin Zurbriggen, are strong rivals to Phil Mahre in the giant slalom. The downhill is almost as open as the special slalom. The course may still be bumpy but two technical sections must be mastered to ensure gold. Although Leonhard Stock, an outsider, won at Lake Placid, the Olympic downhill title usually goes to an established performer capable of mastering his nerves and the occasion. Franz Klammer must be given chance of his second Olympic title to follow 1976, but Harti Weirather, the world champion, Peter Mueller and the Canadians Todd Brooker and Steve Podborski are strongly in the reckoning. Some of the most knowledgeable money may still go on the three relative newcomers – Conradin Cathomen (Switzerland) and Erwin Resch and Helmut Hoeflehner of Austria.

US World Cup winners Phil Mahre and Tamara McKinney seek Olympic gold in Sarajevo

The women's gold medallists may come from a narrower selection. Erika Hess's season was disrupted by injury, but assuming she suffers no further effects she should be strongly in the reckoning for her first Olympic slalom gold medals to follow her two titles in the world championships of 1982. Tamara McKinney, the World Cup overall winner, won three special and four giant slaloms, the best record of any in 1982–3, and must be jointly favoured. The principal challengers are the two veterans, Hanni Wenzel, a double gold and silver medallist at Lake Placid, and, in giant slalom, Irene Epple of West Germany. Italy's Maria Rosa Quario, with two late victories, is a force in special slalom. The retirement of Doris de Agostini leaves the downhill without its World Cup title-holder, but her fellow Swiss, Maria Walliser, showed her qualities in winning the downhill half of the combined in the world championships and won both Megève 1 and Sarajevo to finish joint second to de Agostini. She and Elisabeth Kirchler (Austria), second at Sarajevo and winner of Megève 2, have the qualities for a course with a distinct technical, almost GS, quality in its narrow central section.

Ski Jumping

Malo Polje, Mount Igman
12 February/*70 metres*
18 February/*90 metres*

Ski jumping is based on distance and style. The jumper takes off down a sloping channel called an in-run. Distance is measured from the lip of the take-off to the middle point wher the jumper's feet touch the snow, rounded up to half a metre. Official tables, varying with the Norm point, convert distance into points. Marks are added for style and the highest aggregate for two jumps wins. Judges assess style from the moment flight begins, with a maximum of twenty points. Marks are deducted for bent knees, hips or back, poor body position or improper positioning of skis. The most serious fault is a fall, which, if it occurs on landing, will cost the jumper ten points from each judge, 8–10 points if on a change of gradient, or 20, the maximum, if on the in-run. There are five judges in major competition but the scores of the highest and lowest are removed to eliminate any possibility of bias. The other three marks count.

In a perfect jump the skier should be in a forward leaning position with straight hips (or bending only slightly), with arms at the side or, much less frequently these days, straight ahead. The ideal is to remain motionless and in full control throughout the flight. The jumper should land in a telemark position, that is one foot in front of the other with the knees bent to absorb shock. It is possible for the competitor with the two longest jumps not to win, but it happens rarely these days. A jumper cannot get distance without good style.

Ski jumping attracts huge crowds – more than 100,000 at Oslo's famous Holmenkollen – and is a major television spectacle. Compared with downhill racing it is relatively accident free, partly because its practitioners have built up from small hills and are skilled exponents, partly because falls on steep slopes paradoxically carry less risk than those on flatter slopes. On a 90-metre hill the jumper is 25 to 35 feet above the ground, and flies at about 60–70 mph. In windy or misty conditions the jury has the power to shorten the in-run and reduce risk. Hills are designated according to the length that can safely be jumped and not the physical distance from top to bottom. They are now marked in two places, the Norm (P) and Critical (K) points. The Norm marks the start of the expected landing area, and should not be more than 70 metres or 90 metres from take-off. The Critical point marks the maximum safe landing distance.

In Winter Olympic Games there are separate competitions on the 70- and 90-metre hills, and there is a Nordic combined event doubling cross-country skiing over 15 kilometres with a 70-metre jump. The 70-metre has a smaller tower and a less steep in-run. At Sarajevo the in-runs are side by side and jumpers still land on the same basic slope.

Norway captured fifteen of the possible eighteen jumping medals from the first six Winter Games. Birger Ruud not only took the jumping gold medals of 1932 and 1936, but on the latter occasion also won the downhill, which did not then qualify for a medal, for an amazing double. Finally, in 1948, appointed coach to the Norwegian jumping squad, he came into the team at a late stage to win the silver medal at the age of thirty-six – fourteen years after his first success. Finland, Czechoslovakia, Austria, the USSR and Japan emerged in the following three decades, Japan taking 1–2–3 in the 70-metre at Sapporo. East Germany, with more than 320 synthetic hills, won their first gold through Hans Aschenbach in

Jumping giant: Matti Nykaenen, World Cup overall winner, will be challenged by Horst Bulau (Canada) and Armin Kogler (Austria)

the 70-metre at Innsbruck in 1976. Canada will also have strong contenders at Sarajevo.

Olympic jumping has often provided surprises. At Lake Placid in 1980 Jouko Tormanen, a 25-year-old Laplander who had never won a major event, twice caught a breeze which lifted him to the gold medal. The World Cup series of 1982–3 was won by another Finn, the consistent Matti Nykaenen, who dominated the season together with the Canadian runner-up, Horst Bulau. Nykaenen gained nine first places and Bulau seven. Armin Kogler of Austria, champion for the previous two seasons, gained two of the remaining five first places. A Yugoslav, Primos Ulaga, won the final 90-metre event of the season at Planica, which bodes well for Sarajevo. Nykaenen, Bulau and Kogler must be seen as the favourites.

Cross-country Skiing

Veliko Polje, Mount Igman
Men
10 February/*30 km*
13 February/*15 km*
16 February/*4 × 10 relay*
19 February/*50 km*

Women
9 February/*10 km*
12 February/*5 km*
15 February/*4 × 5 relay*
18 February/*20 km*

Nordic Combined

Malo & Veliko Polje, Mount Igman
11 February/*70-metre jump*
12 February/*15 km*

When the Winter Olympics began in 1924 there were only four ski events, all Nordic. Two involved jumping and two were cross-country races, the 18 (now 15) and 50 kilometres. Both were won by the Norwegian, Thorleif Haug, which was only appropriate. Rock carvings show skiing in Norway and Russia 3,000 years ago. The oldest ski, $3\frac{1}{2}$ feet long and eight inches wide, found at Hoting, Sweden, has been dated by pollen analysis to 2500 BC. Skiing was a means of travel in countries snowbound for at least six months of the year, but the first sporting references to skiing came around 1800 from southern Norway. The first ski races were held at Christiania, now Oslo, and Norwegians were prominent in the export of the sport to Europe and America. Quadrennial Nordic Games, together with the annual Holmenkollen Week, ensured primacy for the Scandinavians through the first quarter of the present century, and the Winter Games were held by them to be a usurper. Alpine skiing was opposed for much the same reasons.

When she finally came to terms with it, Norway dominated Winter Games medal-winning until Lake Placid in 1980, when Russia not only took three of the four men's cross-country events, but overhauled Norway in the tally of gold medals since the first Games at Chamonix – fifty-nine to Norway's fifty. The USSR owed its cross-country tally partly to the introduction of women's events – the 10 kilometres in 1952, the 3 × 5 (now 4 × 5) kilometres in 1956 and the 5 kilometres in 1964. With the introduction of the 20 kilometres at Sarajevo, women have obtained parity with the men in the number of cross-country events run. Norway only recently encouraged women's participation in competitive cross-country, and has only one gold, the relay in 1968, to show. The Russians, although conceding two golds to the East Germans in 1980, have a total of eleven golds out of a potential twenty.

Cross-country skiing, known as *langlauf* in Germany and *langrenn* in Scandinavia, is competitive racing over undulating, prepared ski tracks, the winner being the racer with the fastest time, except in relay events, where the first to finish wins. Participants set off at intervals of 30 seconds, and a passing racer has the right of

Nordic countries no longer have total domination in cross-country

way. An ideal course contains as much uphill as downhill. The technique differs considerably from Alpine skiing. Racers in lightweight suits, sometimes in breeches and stockings, kick with one leg and glide with the other on narrow, lightweight skis, attaining three times the speed of the average good walker over distances varying from 15 kilometres (3 miles) to 50 kilometres (31 miles). Lightweight track shoes are affixed only by toe grips, the heel lifting freely in alternate strides. The basic stride is sometimes alternated with double poling, both poles being set into the ground to push the body forward. The ski is waxed so that the action is much like that of a brush on a wet floor. The ski will glide as long as it is in motion. There may be some straight downhill running where the tracks allow, but the FIS are trying to limit a recent tendency to skate, especially in the start areas, because of the way it chews up the track. The racers start and finish at the same point, but it is a difficult format for television cameras, and the relays produce the best head-to-head challenges.

A linked series of World Cup races was set up in 1981–2, and to many people's surprise it was won by an American, Bill Koch, who had become his country's first Olympic medal winner with a silver in the 30 kilometres at Innsbruck in 1976. Koch held the lead for much of the 1982–3 World Cup series, but in the final event, a 30-kilometre race at Labrador City, Canada, he was ninth and Alexander Zavialov of the Soviet Union won overall by placing second. Gunde Svan of Sweden won the race to pip Koch for second overall. These three, with Jan Lindvall and Lars Erik Eriksen of Norway, and the Lake Placid gold medallists, Thomas Wassberg of Sweden (15 kilometres) and Nikolai Zimiatov of Russia (30 and 50 kilometres), are expected to contend most strongly in Sarajevo.

Marja Liisa Hamalainen of Finland, who won the overall women's World Cup with her outstanding form over the last month, will lead the challenge for the women's Olympic medals. Brit Pettersen of Norway appeared to have an unassailable lead before the Finnish competitor's charge, in which she scored two firsts and two seconds. Kveta Jeriova and Blanka Paulu, both of Czechoslovakia, are also tipped for medals. However the Russian women, led by Lubov Lladova and Raisa Smetanina, 5-kilometre gold medallist at Lake Placid, are likely to raise their game for an Olympics.

Biathlon

Veliko Polje, Mount Igman
11 February/*20 km*
14 February/*10 km*
17 February/*4 × 7.5 km*

The Winter Biathlon, first introduced to the 1960 Squaw Valley Games, is a combination of cross-country skiing and shooting which traces its history to Scandinavian hunting and military patrolling. The 10 and 20 kilometres are individual races with timed starts, and the relay is for four members, each running 7.5 kilometres, with a mass start. The USSR has never lost a relay since it was introduced in 1968, but individual races have been more shared. The Russians have won three of the six 20-kilometre events, but Norway's Magnar Solberg triumphed both at Grenoble and Sapporo. Frank Ullrich took the newly introduced 10-kilometre gold medal in 1980 to mark East Germany's development in the sport.

Competitors in the 20-kilometre race ski looped courses, stopping at four ranges to fire five rounds at falling plate targets. They shoot alternately from a prone and standing position, beginning with prone on the first loop. The target is larger for the standing position (11.5 cm) than for prone (4.5 cm) but the range is always 50 metres. No points are added for hitting the bull's eye, but a shot off target means a one-minute penalty. All penalties are added to the running time. As twenty shots are fired, the maximum penalty is twenty minutes. For example, Victor Arbez of France in 1960 had the fastest time in the 20 kilometres – 1 hour 25:58.4 – but suffered so many shooting penalties that he finished twenty-sixth overall. The winner, Klas Lestender of Sweden, was seven minutes slower than Arbez but hit

Winter biathlon: USSR have not lost a relay since 1968

every target. Anatoli Aljabiev, a lieutenant in the Soviet army, won the gold medal at Lake Placid with a perfect shoot though he was nearly three minutes slower over the 12½ miles than Ullrich, who took second place.

For the 10-kilometre sprint there are two shooting bouts, one prone and the other standing, and a miss entails a penalty loop of 150 metres on a piece of ground adjacent to the range. A penalty loop omitted incurs a two-minute 'fine'. Relay is different in that four members each ski 7.5 kilometres (4½ miles), stopping twice to shoot eight rounds at five breakable targets. At the first, after 3½ kilometres, the skiers fire prone, and at the second, at 5½ kilometres, they are standing. For each unbroken target the relay biathlete must ski a 150-metre penalty loop, which can cost 20–40 seconds. The rifle is a bolt-action .22. Optical sights are forbidden and the minimum trigger pull is 2.2 pounds.

Frank Ullrich remains an outstanding force for Sarajevo having won the World Cup overall in 1981–2. Other gold medal possibilities are the 1983 World Cup winner Peter Angerer of West Germany, Eirik Kvalfoss and Odd Lirhus (Norway), and Anton Schalma (Soviet Union). The Soviet Union, Norway and the two German teams are likely to dispute the relay gold.

Luge

Trebevic

9, 10, 11 and 12 February/*One run daily, Men and Women*
15 February/*Double*

Luge made its entry at the 1964 Innsbruck Olympics and at once gained a grisly notoriety with the death of a Polish-born Briton, Kay Skrzypecki, in practice. It scarcely deserved its reputation as the most dangerous of winter sports. Luge is none other than the ancient sport of tobogganing, practised on everything from a mat to a tin tray since early history. British visitors to Davos in the nineteenth century started sledding on icy roads, and the sports of Cresta Run and bobsleigh spread from that.

The more Germanic form of tobogganing known as luge, or *rodel*, has the rider flat on his or her back, feet forward over the front lip of the sled, head slightly raised. There are no belts or rails to hold the luger on the sled. Unlike the bobsleigh, there is no mechanical steering or braking device. The driver steers by exerting ankle and calf pressures on the forward parts of the runners and by use of shoulder pressure on the toboggan platform. It is a technique learned by trial and error, similar to that used on the Cresta Run at St Moritz, where Britons pioneered tobogganing chest down, head forward on a sliding cradle mounted on runners. The techniques are different, but the objects are the same, to enter and exit out of corners with maximum speed and control, and to accelerate in the straights.

Courses are generally known as *bahns*, from the German way or course, and must be between 1,000 and 1,200 metres long and between 1.35 and 1.50 metres wide. The toboggan is about 5 feet by 18 inches, on steel runners. There are singles and doubles competitions for men, and singles for women, the best aggregate of four runs in singles and two runs in doubles winning. At Trebevic, ten kilometres from the Olympic Village, Sarajevo has built a combined luge and bobsleigh run on the lines of that at Innsbruck.

East Germany gained eight of the available nine medals at Sapporo and five at Innsbruck, but West Germany, Austria, Italy and now Russia are strong in the sport. East Germany took all the men's golds in 1980 but Vera Zozulia set a course record in gaining Russia's first success in luge. The English-speaking world lags far behind. Jeremy Palmer-Tomkinson, twenty-fifth for Britain in the 1968 Grenoble downhill, has competed in three subsequent Olympics in the luge team. It was estimated at Lake Placid that the USA boasted a maximum 200 lugers. When Army Sergeant Volley Cole was first putting a team together in 1964 the qualification was simple. 'All you had to do was call me up.' East and West Germany, Italy and the Soviet Union, with their refrigerated courses constantly available, seem bound to stay ahead in the sport.

Favourites for the men's individual are two Italians, 1980 silver medallist Paul

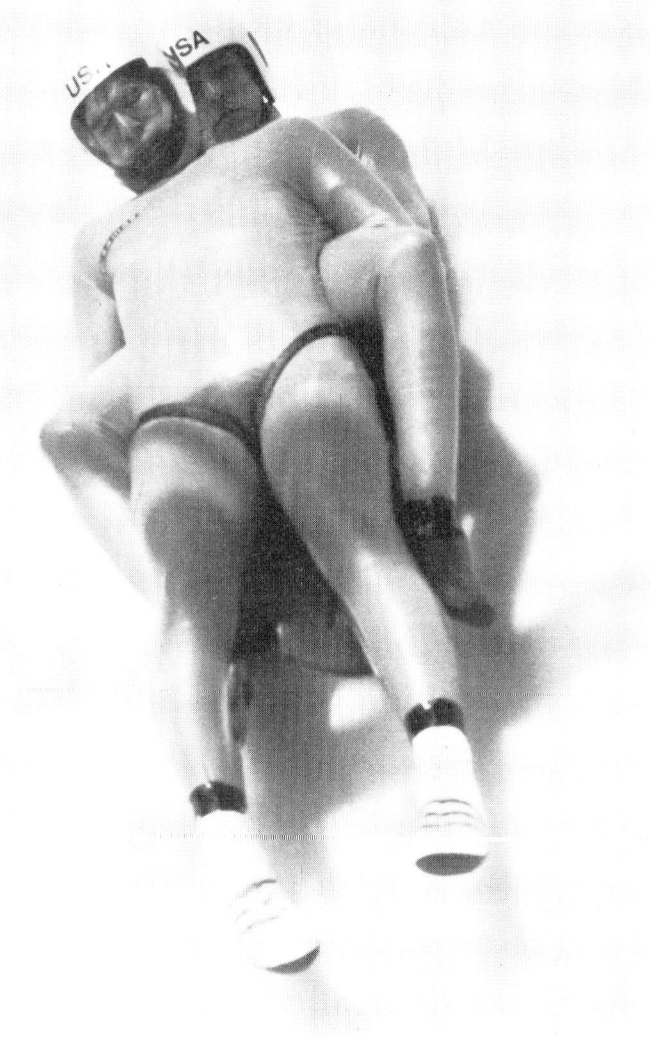

Luge: the ancient sport of tobogganing updated. The Italians are favourites

Hildgartner and Ernst Haspinger, both South Tyrolers experienced in world championships and Olympic luging, Sergei Danelin of the USSR, and the Czech-born world champion, Miroslav Zajonc, now a naturalised Canadian. The women's may be between the 1980 champion Vera Zozulia of the Soviet Union and Bettina Schmidt of East Germany. The doubles favourites are Hans-Jorg Raffl and Norbert Huber of Italy.

Bobsleigh

Trebevic

10, 11 February/*two runs daily, Two-man*
17, 18 February/*two runs daily, Four-man*

Bobsleighing is to ice what Grand Prix motor racing is to roads. The British pioneers at St Moritz soon split into those happy enough to try and control a toboggan through Shuttlecock corner and others seeking more sophisticated means of sliding on ice. The first bobsleigh run was constructed in 1904 on the other side of the road to the Cresta Run, and the simple sleds evolved stage by stage into today's 500-pound racing machines.

In the early years it was in the rules that five-man sleds in fact must include two women. But as the speeds – and the dangers – increased, men were allowed to replace women as ballast. The International Federation of Bobsleigh and Tobogganing was formed in 1923, and bobsleigh was in the first Winter Olympics at Chamonix. In spite of the cost of building runs it has missed out only once since then – at Squaw Valley in 1960. The Yugoslavs are spending £4 million on the combined bob and luge run. There are still critics who say the combined runs are too tame, with too few of the challenges and perils of the 'wall of death' curves built into classic runs, such as those at Cortina, Cervinia, St Moritz and Lake Placid. In trial competition in 1983 Trebevic was found to be challenging enough and, like the downhill ski run, in need of adaptation to make it less dangerous.

A modern bob has the streamlined appearance of a Formula I racing car without aerofoils. The maximum weight for a four-man bob, including crew, is 630 kilos (1,386 lb) and for a two-man bob 390 kilos (860 lb). Lead weight may be added to make up the difference. There are four heats to each event, with the best overall time winning over a course of 1,500 metres.

The British, without success since Tony Nash and Robin Dixon won gold in the 1964 two-man, drafted in top athletes, like the East and West Germans, in an effort to improve the 'push' at the starts. On modern courses fast starting times have proved essential. The bob brakeman and crew must time their shove and jump into the sled perfectly. The driver is the key member, and must know by experience and instinct exactly which line is best for his style and speed. Some will go higher up the concave ice walls than others. Speed of exit from corners is an essential quality.

The USA gained a bobsleigh medal in every Olympics until 1956, but none since. East and West Germany have profited from their refrigerated runs to compete strongly. Meinhard Nehmer, a 39-year-old East German army officer, took his third gold in the four-man at Lake Placid, twice beating one minute in the bobbing equivalent of Roger Bannister's four-minute mile. Nehmer has now retired but fellow East Germans, Bernhard Germeshausen and Horst Schönau, are well capable of piloting their way to Olympic gold, especially in the four-man

Translating St Moritz skills, the Swiss will challenge strongly at Trebevic

event. Their principal rival will be the world champion, Hans Hiltebrand of Switzerland. Another Swiss, the two-man world and Olympic champion, Erik Scharer, will be seeking his second successive title at Sarajevo. Newcomers to watch include Silvio Jubilene (Switzerland) and the Russian, Klaus Kopp.

Ice Hockey

Zetra and **Skenderija**
7, 9, 11, 13, 15, 17 and 19 February

The US ice hockey team's 4–3 defeat of the USSR was a highpoint of the 1980 Lake Placid Games, and the Zetra and Skenderija stadia are bound to provide moments of high drama in the current tournament. Twelve teams are seeded into two groups, with the top two from each five-game round robin taking part in the final play-offs. Group A consists of USSR, Sweden, West Germany, Italy,

Russia, ice hockey champions in four Olympics up to Lake Placid, will be anxious to wipe out defeat by the US

Poland and Yugoslavia, Group B of Czechoslovakia, Canada, Finland, USA, Austria and Norway.

Russia, champions in the four Olympics up to Lake Placid, world champions every year from 1963 except 1972, 1976 and 1977, must once again be favoured. The one team to beat them in World Championships, Czechoslovakia, have yet to win an Olympic title, though taking silver medals in 1948, 1968 and 1976. Canada's six Olympic titles are now old history, their last success being in 1952. The outstanding amateur is now a fossil of Canadian ice hockey history. Every player who rates is now on a professional team's books at the earliest possible age. The Canadian team returning in 1980 after a sixteen-year lapse was made up of university players. The most surprising gold ever was in 1936. Britain won with a team all raised in Canada.

A team at full strength consists of a goalminder and five skaters – a three-man forward line with a centre and two wings, and two defencemen, using curved sticks to try and propel a vulcanised rubber puck through a goal 1.83 metres (6 ft) wide and 1.22 metres (4 ft) high. A maximum of eighteen players plus two goalminders is allowed per team. There are three twenty-minute periods, with the clock stopped when play halts. Teams change ends at the start of each period and midway through the third period. Infractions such as holding, tripping, high sticking, boarding and cross-checking incur two-minute penalties in the 'sin bin'. If the opposing team scores during a two-minute ban the player is allowed to return immediately. A five-minute ban may be imposed for serious offences such as fighting, and the player must serve the full time regardless of goals. The goalminder may be substituted for an attacking skater if a team is seeking an equaliser towards the finish. A minor penalty incurred by a goalminder may be served by a team-mate.

Two blue lines divide the rink into three zones, and no attacking player can precede the puck into the furthest zone without penalty of offside and a face-off, in which the puck is dropped between two players. The face-off is the normal means of restarting play. The puck cannot be sent from one end of the ice to the other without being touched or carried by an attacking player. A pass from a defence zone must be picked up before it crosses the red halfway line.

Speed Skating

Zetra

Men	Women
10 February/*500 m*	9 February/*1,500 m*
12 February/*5,000 m*	10 February/*500 m*
14 February/*1,000 m*	13 February/*1,000 m*
16 February/*1,500 m*	15 February/*3,000 m*
18 February/*10,000 m*	

Speed skating is the fastest of all sports over a level surface. In the shorter races men skaters average almost 30 mph. The 111.89-metre straight of a 400-metre outdoor oval – the standard rink – is covered in eight or nine strides. Over 1,500 metres the speed skater is nearly two minutes faster than Sebastian Coe.

In no other sport is an athlete encouraged to be talented in all its distances. International meetings other than Olympic Games usually last two days, the 500 and 5,000 metres on the first and 1,500 and 10,000 metres on the second, with draw placements based on performance, and the skaters racing two at a time against the clock. Only the best sixteen skate the 10,000. At an Olympic Games there is a fifth event, the 1,000 metres, so five gold medals are available. Eric Heiden of the USA, from Madison, Wisconsin, reared on America's only 400-metre outdoor rink at West Allis, in the same state, won all five gold medals at Lake Placid. Heiden was the outstanding individual of the Games. He retired to

Fastest over a level surface: speed-skating medals may go to Russians and East Germans after Eric Heiden's domination

go into sports medicine on winning the 10,000 metres on the final Saturday in the world record time of 14:28.13, more than six seconds faster than the record set by Viktor Leskin of the USSR at Alma Ata in 1977, and more than fifteen seconds faster than his previous best. Only one other man, Ivar Ballangrud of Norway in 1936, had ever won both the Olympic 500 and 10,000 metres. It was a performance which may not be equalled in a long time.

Speed skating is believed to date from the twelfth century in Holland, but the first all-iron skates were fashioned in Scotland in the sixteeth century and the first organised races took place there. The Skating Club of Edinburgh was formed in 1642 and the activity spread to Northern Europe, and Holland in particular. A Dutchman, Jaap Eden, won the first World Speed Championship in 1893 over the classic distances of 500, 1,500, 5,000 and 10,000 metres. The sport developed strongly in Norway, with distinct semi-professional undertones. Women's events were introduced to the Olympics in 1960, when Lydia Skoblikova, a blonde, blue-eyed Siberian schoolteacher, won two gold medals. She went on to take all four at Innsbruck in 1964, setting world records in three.

Lake Placid also saw an all-American triumph in 1932, but this was the one and only time the Olympics staged mass-start races in which North Americans alone specialised. In regular competition skaters are drawn to race against the clock two at a time around the 400-metre track. There is an obvious advantage in being drawn against a better skater, for it introduces an element of competition. The draw is conducted in seeded groups depending on recent form. The standard track has two lanes each five metres wide and one straight is a designated crossing area where the skaters change lanes after each circuit. It is the responsibility of the racer leaving the inner lane to avoid collision.

The world's fastest times in 1983 were all set by Russians or East Germans at Alma Ata, the Soviet rink with notably fast ice. More pertinently perhaps, Rolf Falk-Larssen of Norway won the world championship in Oslo and Andrea Schöne of East Germany won the women's world title at Karl Marx Stadt. All the same, it will be a surprise if Soviet and East German skaters do not pick up a large haul of medals. Favourite in the 500 and 1,000 metres men's is Pavel Pegov, and fellow Russians Igor Zhelesovksk (1,500 metres), Anatoli Kaputin (3,000), Sergei Pribitkov (5,000) and Konstantin Korotkov (10,000) all set fastest times in 1983. Andrea Schöne is especially strong over 3,000 and 5,000 metres. Christa Rothenburger, a fellow East German, is best over 500 metres, and a Russian, Natalia Petruseva, over 1,000 and 1,500 metres.

Figure Skating

Zetra and **Skenderija**
10, 12 February/*Pairs*
10, 12, 14 February/*Dance*
13, 14, 16 February/*Men*
15, 16, 18 February/*Women*

Figure skating has become a major world television spectacular in the last two decades, but it has a long and distinguished history as a competitive sport which is also a genuine art form. Sixteen years before the first Winter Games it was welcomed to the London Summer Games of 1908, and Britain's Madge Syers-Cave, who had shocked the establishment by entering the otherwise all-male World Championship five years before, was the first woman champion. It is the one winter-associated sport in which Britain has truly excelled, Jeannette Altwegg in 1952, John Curry in 1976 and Robin Cousins in 1980 all gaining gold. It will be a major surprise if Jayne Torvill and Christopher Dean fail to make it a fifth British gold medal. Ice dancing would almost certainly have provided Britain with more golds, but it was only recognised as an Olympic event in 1976.

Torvill and Dean: the shock of the Games if they don't win

There are four Olympic events, men's and women's singles, pair and dance, each comprising compulsory and freestyle sections. In recent years more emphasis has been put on the freestyle form, and a new category, the short programme, has been introduced to singles. Where at one time school figures in singles counted 60 per cent of the total score, now they are worth 30 per cent. The freestyle has been boosted from 40 to 50 per cent, and now the short programme counts 20 per cent. In July 1980 the International Skating Union changed its scoring system, whereby the skater's finish place in each section – school figures, short programme and free – is multiplied by a factor. These numbers are added together, with the skater winning who has the lowest number of 'penalty points'. In the case of a tie the skater placed higher in the free skating is given the higher place. Ice dancing has similar categories known as compulsory, original set pattern and free, and the same basic scoring system applies. School figures and compulsory dances are worth 30 per cent of the total and the factor is 0.6. The short programmes and original set patterns are worth 20 per cent and the factor is 0.4. The free skating and dancing are worth 50 per cent and the factor is 1.0. When Torvill and Dean won all three sections in the 1983 World Championships they received the best possible penalty points – 2.0 – which were computed as compulsory dance 1 × 0.6; set pattern 1 × 0.4; and free 1 × 1.

School figures require the tracing of patterns based on the figure eight. The short programme, or compulsory freestyle, requires seven free-skating elements such as spins, jumps and combinations, set to two minutes of music. The freestyle, over four minutes for women and four and a half for men, is devised by the individual and coach to incorporate elements and music of their choice. The judges mark on both technical merit and artistic impression, so skaters going for medals must attempt the most difficult programme. The judges mark to a maximum of six in individual assessment, but the computation of results is worked out in ordinals – a skater's place in relation to the others – and points.

Pair skating has a short programme lasting two minutes 15 seconds of compulsory moves which count approximately 35 per cent, and four and a half minutes of free skating. The short programme is designed around seven moves, and the free should consist of both slow and fast music, including lifts, jumps, spins and connecting steps all in unison and harmony. Ice dancing requires a similar unison but is more regimented, in its pure skating form.

The favourite in the men's singles is Scott Hamilton (USA), world title-holder since 1981. The women's is more open, with Rosalynn Sumners (USA), the world champion, and Katarina Witt (East Germany) the principal contenders. The pairs will be between the 1983 champions Elena Valova and Oleg Vasiliev (USSR), East Germans Sabine Baess and Tassilo Thierbach, and Barbara Underhill and Paul Martini of Canada.

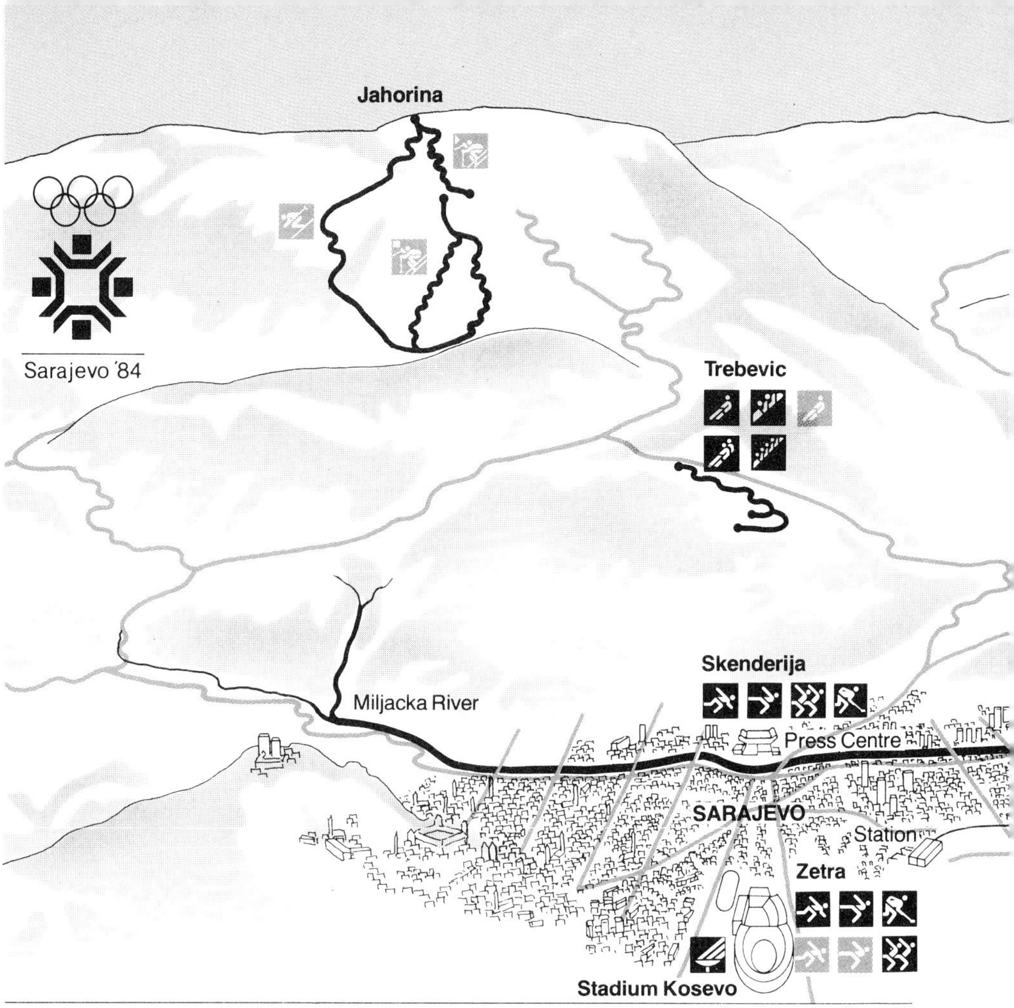

Jahorina

Sarajevo '84

Trebevic

Skenderija

Miljacka River

Press Centre

SARAJEVO

Station

Zetra

Stadium Kosevo

OLYMPIC GAMES CALENDAR FEBRUARY 1984

7 TUESDAY	SKENDERIJA 1 13.00/16.30/20.00	VELIKO POLJE, IGMAN 20km 9.00-12.00	TREBEVIC 4 Run 9.00-11.00
ZETRA 13.30/17.00/20.30	**10 FRIDAY**	TREBEVIC 3 Run 9.00-11.00	ZETRA 5000m 9.30-12.30
SKENDERIJA 1 13.00/16.30/20.00	VELIKO POLJE, IGMAN 30km 9.00-11.30	TREBEVIC 3 Run 9.00-11.00	ZETRA OSP D 14.00-18.00
8 WEDNESDAY	TREBEVIC 2 Run 9.00-11.00	TREBEVIC 3-4 Run 13.30-16.00	ZETRA FS P 19.30-23.00
STADIUM KOSEVO 14.30-16.00	TREBEVIC 2 Run 9.00-11.00	JAHORINA 10.30-12.30	**13 MONDAY**
9 THURSDAY	TREBEVIC 1-2 Run 13.30-16.00	ZETRA 13.30/17.00/20.30	VELIKO POLJE, IGMAN 15km 9.00-10.40
VELIKO POLJE, IGMAN 10km 9.00-10.00	ZETRA 500m 9.30-10.30	SKENDERIJA 1 13.00/16.30/20.00	ZETRA 1000m 9.30-11.00
BJELASNICA 12.00-14.00	ZETRA 500m 11.00-12.00	**12 SUNDAY**	SKENDERIJA 2 CF 7.00-15.00
TREBEVIC 1 Run 9.00-11.00	ZETRA CD1 14.00-18.00	MALO POLJE, IGMAN 70m 13.00-15.00	ZETRA 13.30/17.00/20.30
TREBEVIC 1 Run 9.00-11.00	ZETRA SP P 20.00-23.00	VELIKO POLJE, IGMAN 15km 12.00-14.00	SKENDERIJA 1 13.00/16.30/20.00
ZETRA 1.500m 9.30-11.30	**11 SATURDAY**	VELIKO POLJE, IGMAN 5km 9.00-9.40	**14 TUESDAY**
ZETRA 13.30/17.00/20.30	MALO POLJE, IGMAN 70m 12.30-14.30	TREBEVIC 4 Run 9.00-11.00	VELIKO POLJE, IGMAN 10km 9.00-12.00

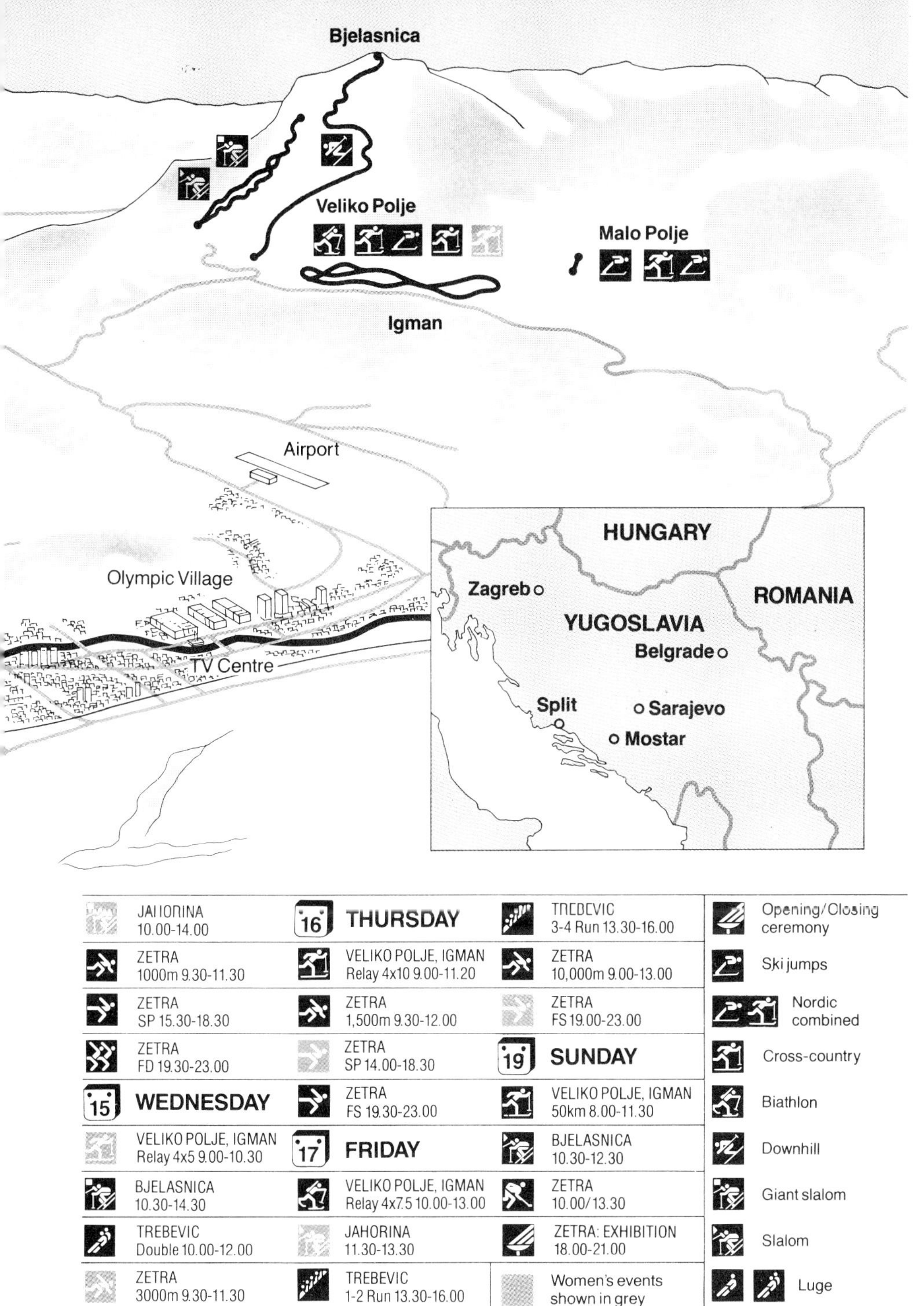

JAHORINA
10.00-14.00

ZETRA
1000m 9.30-11.30

ZETRA
SP 15.30-18.30

ZETRA
FD 19.30-23.00

15 WEDNESDAY

VELIKO POLJE, IGMAN
Relay 4x5 9.00-10.30

BJELASNICA
10.30-14.30

TREBEVIC
Double 10.00-12.00

ZETRA
3000m 9.30-11.30

SKENDERIJA 2
CF 7.00-16.00

ZETRA
13.30/17.00/20.30

SKENDERIJA 1
13.00/16.30/20.00

16 THURSDAY

VELIKO POLJE, IGMAN
Relay 4x10 9.00-11.20

ZETRA
1,500m 9.30-12.00

ZETRA
SP 14.00-18.30

ZETRA
FS 19.30-23.00

17 FRIDAY

VELIKO POLJE, IGMAN
Relay 4x7.5 10.00-13.00

JAHORINA
11.30-13.30

TREBEVIC
1-2 Run 13.30-16.00

ZETRA
13.30/17.00/20.30

18 SATURDAY

MALO POLJE, IGMAN
90m 12.30-15.00

VELIKO POLJE, IGMAN
20km 9.00-12.00

TREBEVIC
3-4 Run 13.30-16.00

ZETRA
10,000m 9.00-13.00

ZETRA
FS 19.00-23.00

19 SUNDAY

VELIKO POLJE, IGMAN
50km 8.00-11.30

BJELASNICA
10.30-12.30

ZETRA
10.00/13.30

ZETRA: EXHIBITION
18.00-21.00

Women's events shown in grey

OSP D	Original short programme (Dance)
CD	Compulsory dance
FD	Free dance
SP P	Short programme (Pairs)
FS P	Free skating (Pairs)
CF	Compulsory figures
SP	Short programme
FS	Free skating

Opening/Closing ceremony
Ski jumps
Nordic combined
Cross-country
Biathlon
Downhill
Giant slalom
Slalom
Luge
Bobsleigh
Speed skating
Figure skating
Ice hockey

3

FROM CHAMONIX TO LAKE PLACID

The Story of the Winter Games

When a downhiller as daring and macho as Franz Klammer could admit that he backed off a jump, as he did in the final hump of the pre-Olympic downhill track at Sarajevo, then it was certain that a Winter Olympic Games was again on course for controversy. Downhill courses are a major source of trouble. It is not simply that men and women flat out on three-inch-wide boards are unusually selective. They are entitled, they feel, to distinguish between humps they can swallow at 80 mph and those that throw them dangerously and unfairly. The organisers took due note and promised a better configuration for the downhill which, with a proper sense of the theatrical, opens every Winter Games. Three days of intensive bulldozer work, they believed, could put it right. The Yugoslavs at least have a genuine course, even if it does have to start on a restaurant roof to achieve the minimum vertical drop required by the FIS.

In 1976 Denver was forced to give up the Games partly because the downhill course was projected in a national park area, drawing down the wrath of environmentalists. In 1972, at Sapporo, Japan, Mount Eniwa, a virgin mountain of 4,000 feet spangled with silver birches, was given two downhill courses by 15,000 men, 850 bulldozers and six tons of explosive. In addition it was draped with two cable cars capable of transporting 330 people an hour, and a chair lift. Within weeks of the finish of the Games it was returned to its original pristine state. Sapporo's Otaru Park annually stages a Snow Sculpture with creatures of legend sculpted in ice and snow, and brilliantly coloured flowers in showcases of diamond-like ice – all magically there and gone in a matter of days. But Eniwa's £2 million disappearing trick found no appreciative applause from Avery Brundage, president of the IOC. He saw it only as one more shameful excess by the winter sports industry. Denver, he hoped, would give the Winter Games a decent burial. In fact Innsbruck took them over with almost indecent alacrity. Whether ski racers were full- or part-time professionals was becoming a matter of arcane debate. Too many countries wanted the Winter Olympics for reasons of business or national prestige. The expulsion of Karl Schranz of Austria from the Sapporo Games laid open a festering wound. He was merely the most vocal of Brundage's critics, saying that the Winter Games should be for the best, not the best-heeled, athletes.

Brundage's attitude was largely personal. Lord Killanin, who succeeded him as president after the 1972 Munich Games, held a far more liberal approach. The movement had been brought face to face with much more violent problems by the Black September attack on the Israeli team at Munich. Among societies devoting much more time to sport and recreation, definitions of amateurism became steadily more irrelevant. Eastern Europeans paid lip service to amateurism because they had state rather than commercial sponsorship of competitors, and few recognised professionals. The West had all manner of athletes released by their companies for an unlimited period of time. Killanin and the IOC more and more took the view that, rather than impose a draconian rule on amateurism, international federations should set their own rules and standards, and Rule 26 to this effect was passed at the IOC Vienna meeting in October 1974. Skiing, show jumping and sailing clearly required more expensive artefacts than running. Skiing, in addition, involved the tourist trade in a number of influential countries. The FIS had to come to terms with the situation, which it did by channelling equipment and other commercial cash through pools controlled by national federations. Full-time racers were rewarded according to standings and performance, though clearly some made personal contracts, usually undisclosed. Ingemar Stenmark, the world's leading slalom skier, winner of the overall World Cup three times, after the 1980 Lake Placid Winter Games openly made personal arrangements under a 'B' licence system finally retracted by the FIS at its 1983 congress in Sydney. The FIS demanded that Stenmark transfer all his funds from Monte Carlo to a Swedish ski federation account in Sweden before he could compete at Sarajevo. Poor Stenmark protested that the Swedish tax men would take 90 per cent of his money.

FIS had found the operation of a dual professional and broken-time system (the reimbursement of an athlete for income he might have received) too difficult to administer. The recession of the late 1970s and the 1980s exposed the relatively narrow financial base of skiing. Outstanding winners might benefit substantially. Anyone else was struggling. When the Canadian ski federation got into financial trouble in 1983 and imposed levies on its skiers, including A team members like the World Cup downhill title-holder Steve Podborski, even those able to finish in the top twenty could not find the £1,000 to pay, and commercial interests had to step in. It was not only a matter of principle for the racers. Their trust funds had not built up to look after the sudden expense.

Winter Games are not only about money, materials and amateur–professional disputes, but they do tend to highlight the problems of wealthier countries. Recreation on mountains at 5,000 to 10,000 feet can be hazardous and costly, with the need for specialist equipment and clothing. Artificial snow and ice are expensive to install. In the late 1970s most US ski resorts, including those high in the Rockies, invested in man-made snow. American experts calculated that it cost about \$2,000 (£1,350) to cover a trail 3,000 feet long and 15 feet wide with one six-inch application of snow, which multiplied up represents a huge outlay. However, if trade drops by \$287.7 million because of a natural snow famine, as happened in Colorado in 1980–1, an expense of \$20 million is justified.

So instinctive is the desire to slide on ice and snow, and to develop skill and pleasure in doing so, that no other justification really need be sought for a Winter Olympics. Jet transport and increasing leisure time have opened up the whole concept of winter recreation to people who live far from the snow. And though the sports of the Winter Games are primarily for doers rather than watchers, skilled exploitation of the cameras has revolutionised televiewing. More than 500 million people watch the Games of modern times. There are many reasons for their ever-growing popularity. Winter sports have a long history of participation by both sexes. In 1768–9 Casanova relates how he donned skates to pursue a high-society maiden. Alpine skiing has encouraged women from the first. The Scandinavian countries preserved a chilly conservatism to the original concept of the Winter Games, deeming the Nordic Games much more important and for long denying the legitimacy of Alpine, or downhill only, skiing. But in 1952 in Oslo, the heartland of Nordic skiing, women contested a 10-kilometre cross-country race for the first time.

Winter Games are also exceptional in encouraging both the physical and the aesthetic. Thus skiing was once marked on style points. Ski jumping still is, though it is rare these days that the longest jumps do not win. Figure skating contains an essential measure of subjective judgement. Ice hockey retains a male, macho image, as does ski jumping, but not speed skating, which introduced women's events in 1960. Tobogganing was next, with the first women's events in 1964. American research shows that women notably boost the viewing figures of major sporting occasions. This certainly applies to the Winter Games, and it is appropriate that winter sports generally are in the van of women's participation.

I Chamonix 1924

Anyone who believes that the world's climate has changed for the worse only in the last few years should look at the history of Winter Olympic Games. Most have been disrupted or threatened by the weather, and Chamonix in 1924 was no exception. On 23 December the resort, until then famous only for its mountaineering tradition, prayed for a white Christmas as never before. The town had volunteered to hold the first experimental Winter Games, but with a month to go not a flake of snow had fallen at lower altitudes. On 24 December the citizens awoke to 1.10 metres (3 ft 8 in) of it. As much as 36,000 square metres had to be cleared from the skating rink, mostly by bent back and shovel load, since snow ploughs did not exist. A week before the start, rain turned the ice rink into a lake. But on the eve of events a hard frost set in and the Games were saved. The 294 competitors from sixteen countries took part in fourteen events, the pioneers being: Austria, Belgium, Canada, Czechoslovakia, Finland, France, Great Britain, Hungary, Italy, Latvia, Norway, Poland, Sweden, Switzerland, the United States and Yugoslavia. Women were eligible only for figure skating and no Alpine skiing was held at all.

Norway, whose opposition to the Games had been longest and strongest, provided the first major hero – Thorleif Haug, who won three gold medals in the 18 kilometres and 50 kilometres cross-country skiing, and the Nordic combination. He also took a bronze in the special jumping. Norway also took the most celebrated last place in the first of the Games. The blonde and winsome Sonja Henie, who a few weeks earlier had won her national championships at the age of ten, finished last in the women's skating but created the first enduring impression of a career which was to embrace three gold medals and worldwide Hollywood fame.

The ice-rink was the principal arena of the Games as Gillis Grafstrom of Sweden earned the second of three figure-skating gold medals – figure skating had been absorbed into the Olympics as early as 1908 – and Canada successfully defended the ice-skating title won for the first time at Antwerp in 1920. The Finn, Clas Thunberg, became the first speed skater to take home a rich haul of medals with golds in the 1,500 and 5,000 metres, silver in the 10,000 and bronze in the 500 metres.

II St Moritz 1928

The Netherlands staged the Summer Games in Amsterdam, but were unable to provide anything other than pancake-flat skating rinks for a Winter Games. St Moritz, long renowned as a ski resort, readily stepped in. The Swiss were accustomed to the sight of girls in plus fours and monocles and men wearing grass skirts and skis. What came much harder was the *föhn*, a warm wind from the south. On the morning of the 50-kilometre cross-country the skiers waxed at a temperature of minus 17.8°C (0°F). By the afternoon, despite St Moritz's altitude of 1,850 metres (6,066 feet), the thermometer had soared to 25°C (77°F). A quarter of the racers retired, such was the sweltering heat, from this marathon of skiing. Swedish skill and luck saw them to all three medals, though Per Erik Hedlund's winning time was almost 70 minutes slower than Haug's in Chamonix.

It rained all day and night on 15 February, wiping out any competition, but as quickly as it came the *föhn* went. A hard frost set into the molten snow, and the Games were saved. Grafstrom achieved his third and last figure-skating gold medal; Sonja Henie, not yet sixteen, earned her first. The US won both the five-man bob and the tobogganing on the Cresta Run, but the British, too, enjoyed success of a different order. During the Games, Arnold Lunn persuaded the FIS to include downhill and slalom experimentally in international competition. Alpine skiing had at last overcome the Scandinavian objections, but it was eight

And the last shall be first: Sonja Henie, aged 11, finished last in the figure skating at Chamonix, but won St Moritz aged 15, the first of three golds

long years before it took its place in an Olympic Games, and twenty more before, at the post-war St Moritz Games, a gold medal was awarded for both downhill and slalom separately.

III Lake Placid 1932

The Winter Olympics crossed the Atlantic for the first time when Lake Placid, New York State, a newly-established resort close to the Canadian border, staged them at the heart of the great Depression. Only 568 metres (1,862 ft) high, and subject to the weather extremes of the North American continent, Lake Placid had to import snow by the truckload from Canada to help repair the cross-country tracks. Europeans scoffed at the time, though in later years the whole winter sports world came to respect the need for snow-making and shifting to defeat variable conditions and honour television schedules.

Innovation abounded. Figure skating was held indoors for the first time and Sonja Henie spellbound an American audience as she had a Swiss. A superstar was in orbit. Americans and Canadians, enjoying massed-start speed skating, took ten of the twelve available medals, to European discomfiture. The World Championships were held on the same rink soon afterwards, and under the more customary practice of timed starting in pairs, the Norwegian, Ivar Ballangrud, won the 1,500, 5,000 and 10,000 metres.

In bobsleigh, Germany II insisted on a bob with rounded as opposed to hollow-ground runners and finished up in a wood with the four-man crew requiring hospital treatment. It was replaced by an American bob with a team recruited from Germans living in the USA untrained as serious bobbers. US teams took the two-man and four-man gold medals, while the German-Americans escaped with their lives.

The special ski jump suffered a rainstorm then a hard frost. On the outrun of the jump hill a small pool remained into which jumpers took an involuntary bath. Soaked participants complained furiously but unavailingly as they waited their turn for second jumps on the open tower whipped by bitter winds. The FIS champion, Birger Ruud, of Norway, overcame all the handicaps sublimely to win his first Olympic jumping gold medal.

IV Garmisch-Partenkirchen 1936

Nazi anxiety to gain world recognition, and the staging of a Winter Games near large population centres, brought the first mass publicity and major following to the Winter Olympics. The Swiss team resolutely refused to give the Nazi salute at the opening ceremony in spite of the presence of Adolf Hitler. There were 755 competitors from twenty-eight countries and half a million paying spectators, with trains leaving Munich every ten minutes throughout the night and many thousands more coming from Innsbruck, for a Games notable for the introduction of Alpine ski racing. The Nazis literally had the luck of the devil with the weather, persistent rain threatening to ruin events until the very eve of the Games, when low-level Garmisch suddenly revelled in snow and sub-zero temperatures. Rain returned as soon as the Games were finished.

The special ski jump, the concluding event, was watched by 150,000 people – still a record. It was won by Birger Ruud of Norway, the FIS world champion, who earlier had won the first Olympic downhill. Ruud had been a frequent business visitor to Austria and Switzerland, but his Alpine victory was still extraordinary. In the first of many disputes with FIS, the IOC ruled out ski teachers from taking part, though FIS permitted them to race as amateurs in their own competitions. The 16-year-old Laila Schou-Nilsen, another Norwegian, better known as a speed skater and tennis player, won the women's downhill for a remarkable Norwegian double, the more ironic for Norway's long and often bitter rejection of Alpine skiing. The first downhill had been held by the British Kandahar Club twenty-five years earlier. Another irony was the success of the German team in the slaloms, their full-time squad training introducing the concept of state

Nazis hail British at Garmisch: the Britons were instructed to hold an arm out sideways, the official Olympic salute, in reply

athletes. Franz Pfnür won the men's and Christl Cranz the women's, and both took the gold medal for their overall performances. Individual medals for the Alpine events were not introduced until 1948.

Ivar Ballangrud of Norway took three speed-skating gold medals and a silver, and Sonja Henie her third figure-skating gold in successive Olympics. The Canadians, victors in each of the Olympic ice hockey tournaments hitherto, were beaten 2–1 by a British team made up of British-born Canadians, and though

Double of doubles: Norway's Birger Ruud wins his second jumping gold to go with the men's downhill at Garmisch

they drew 0–0 with the United States the British took the gold medal on the strength of Canada's defeat of the USA 1–0.

The IOC adopted Sapporo as the 1940 venue but Japan waived the claim because of the Sino-Japanese war. In June 1939, the IOC accepted Garmisch's offer to restage the Games and although the Second World War began on 3 September German preparations went on until 22 November 1939, when they finally wound up their organisation.

V St Moritz 1948

The emergence of Alpine ski racing as the major event of a Winter Games coincided with the postwar pattern of splitting the Summer and Winter Games between different countries. In 1948 London staged the Summer Games and St Moritz the Winter. Although Germany and Japan were not admitted, twenty-eight countries competed – the same as at Garmisch-Partenkirchen – with 636 men and 77 women competitors. The postwar mood was caught by Gretchen Fraser of the

Time to celebrate: pig-tailed Gretchen Fraser of America won the women's slalom at St Moritz – at the age of 29

USA as, pigtails flying, she won the slalom. She was all of twenty-nine years old. Henri Oreiller of France gained most ski gold medals with victories in the downhill and combination and a bronze in the special slalom. Giant slalom was not added until four years later. Sadly, Oreiller was to die in a motor racing accident at Montlhéry in 1962. The O-K piste of the Val d'Isère downhill is still named after him and Killy. This was the first occasion the FIS awarded World Championship medals simultaneously with Olympic.

A *föhn* once again ensured a weather disruption, and ice hockey matches and the 10,000 metres speed skating were postponed because of poor ice, but the Games were generally a joyous celebration of peace. John R. Heaton, USA, won the silver on the Cresta Run twenty years after gaining second place to his brother, Jennison; Birger Ruud took the silver in the 70-metre ski jump sixteen years after his first Olympic victory and twelve after his second. Norwegians took all three medals on account of their style. The winner, Petter Hugstedt, was

Olympic spirit: Jeannette Altwegg won the women's figure skating at Oslo but declined all ice-show offers to help a children's village

outjumped by both the Finn, Matti Pietikainen, and the American, Gordon Wren. Norway retained speed-skating dominance, winning three of the four races, but although Canada regained the hockey title, the European challenge emerged with Czechoslovakia beaten only on goal average.

VI Oslo 1952

Norway, the arch opponent of Olympic Games and the homeland of skiing, at last was the host and a sense of occasion marked every event. A total of 561,407 people watched the festivities and nearly 130,000 saw a Norwegian, Arnfinn Bergmann, win the Holmenkollen ski jump in a magnificent climax.

The Games opened with the lighting of the flame in the Bislett Stadium by Eigil Nansen, grandson of the explorer Fridtjof Nansen, whose book, *The First*

Crossing of Greenland (1890), inspired skiing throughout Europe. Another Norwegian, Stein Eriksen, was the star of the men's Alpine skiing, winning the newly-introduced giant slalom and taking the special slalom silver medal. It was a performance even bettered by the 19-year-old Andrea Mead-Lawrence in women's skiing. On the first day of competition she won the giant slalom, collapsing into the arms of her husband at the finish, then after falling twice in the downhill to finish seventeenth she came back dramatically to win the special slalom.

Hjalmar Anderson further delighted Norwegians by winning the 1,500-, 5,000- and 10,000-metre speed skating. Richard Button of the USA, introducing the first triple rotation jump, won the men's figure skating, and Jeannette Altwegg, of Britain, having won the women's, rejected all offers to join ice shows to help run the Pestalozzi Children's Village in Switzerland. Germany won the two- and four-man bobsleigh events, but with such heavyweight crews that the International Bobsleigh Federation was subsequently persuaded to introduce weight limits.

VII Cortina d'Ampezzo 1956

Cortina set more landmarks for winter sports. It was the first widely televised Games. The Russians, entered for the first time, won the ice hockey and excelled in speed-skating; and Anton (Toni) Sailer became Alpine skiing's pin-up boy, until superseded by Jean-Claude Killy in 1968, by taking all three gold medals.

Sailer, a handsome 20-year-old Kitzbueheler, won the Alpine events by extraordinary margins – the giant slalom by 6.2 seconds, the special slalom by 4.0, and the downhill by 3.5. He became the fifth winter sportsman to win three medals at a Games, the others being the Scandinavians Thorleif Haug, Clas Thunderberg, Ivar Ballangrud and Hjalmar Anderson. The effect on the Austrian tourist industry was enormous, and overnight he became a film star.

Finland eclipsed Norway in the ski jumping, their new style, with arms held to their sides instead of forwards like a diver, proving much more effective aerodynamically. Franz Kapus (Switzerland) at forty-six became the oldest gold-medal winner in piloting the four-man bob to victory. The USA dominated the skating, taking five of the medals, with Hayes Alan Jenkins and Tenley Albright the king and queen of the ice.

VIII Squaw Valley 1960

An isolated Californian mountain in the Sierra Nevada hosted the eighth Games to set another precedent. It was the first purpose-built ski centre to stage a Games and was a monument to the initiative and industry of Alexander Cushing, who persuaded the IOC by 32 votes to 30 to choose it before Innsbruck. Walt Disney

Ski pin-up: Toni Sailer won three golds at Cortina, then went into films. He was banned from Squaw Valley in 1960 because a firm selling Toni Sailer ski pants mentioned his Olympic success in their ads

took charge of the opening-day ceremony with a 2,000-voice choir and 1,000-piece band playing the Olympic hymn. Snow White would perhaps have been more appropriate than Vice President Richard Nixon to open the Games, more so since a severe snowstorm disrupted affairs, but good weather prevailed for the eleven days of competition. Complaints over the altitude, 2,000 metres (6,650 ft), for the cross-country events and the refusal to build a bob run for only nine interested countries were soon overborne by the genuine pleasure of a Games run as a 'village' event, with competitors in close touch and with no communication or transport problems.

The Alpine ski honours were shared around, in contrast to Cortina. Switzerland was the only country to win two events, but all the figure-skating gold medals went to the USA. The Americans also won the ice hockey, an indication – which Lake Placid in 1980 was to confirm – that in team sports the home country enjoys considerable psychological and logistical advantages.

The Russians did not do quite as well as expected, but still took seven gold

Six golds: Lydia Skoblikova of the Soviet Union won two women's speed-skating golds at Squaw Valley. Four years later at Innsbruck she took four more

medals in the twenty-seven events, Lydia Skoblikova winning two in the newly-introduced women's speed-skating. Biathlon, a 20-kilometre cross-country ski race interspersed with four series of rifle shooting tests, was also introduced over the heads of critics who claimed it was a military exercise. Klas Lestander of Sweden was the first gold medallist. His fellow countryman, Sixten Jernberg, continued an illustrious cross-country career with victory in the 30-kilometre, and Georg Thoma of Germany became the first non-Scandinavian to win the Nordic combined (15-kilometre cross-country and 70-metre jumping).

IX Innsbruck 1964

Austria's first welcome to the Winter Olympics was complete in almost every detail except the snow. The country which, through pioneers such as Matthew Zdarsky and Hannes Schneider, felt as proprietorial towards Alpine skiing as the English about cricket had 3,000 soldiers shovelling and dumping furiously to preserve the previous white arteries of ski trails on bare mountainsides.

Innsbruck set many precedents. It was the first of a series of big cities to stage an Olympic Games. Not only pride but a tourist industry heavily supportive of the Austrian economy rode on events. Satellite centres were up to fifteen miles

Russian pioneers: Oleg Protopopov and Ludmila Belousova took the first-ever Soviet figure-skating gold at Innsbruck

from the city, but transport problems were solved with major effort and enterprise. Innsbruck welcomed a record 1,186 competitors and more than a million spectators. The Austrian authorities spent nearly £12 million on the Games and IBM another £500,000 to ensure that results such as the figure skating, which took eight hours to work out at Cortina, were computered into press centres within seconds. Never before had a Games attracted such publicity, media people far outnumbering competitors and thirty-four television networks represented.

Avery Brundage, president of the IOC, protested at the commercialism of ski-racers displaying their equipment before the cameras. A new world was opening up in which the old amateur codes were to be substantially redefined. The Soviet Union's heavily state-subsidised athletes took eleven events, but seven were from two women schoolteachers, the 24-year-old Lydia Skoblikova, who took all four speed-skating gold medals in four days, and Claudia Boyarskikh, 23, who won the 5- and 10-kilometres cross-country races and gained further gold in the 15-kilometres relay. Women took a prominent part, with the Goitschel sisters of France duelling for gold and silver. Marielle won the GS with Christine second, the positions being reversed for the special slalom. For Austrians there is only one ski race – the men's downhill. Egon Zimmerman won that, so they were happy, but Christl Haas added the bonus of the women's downhill. The Russian skaters, Oleg Protopopov and Ludmila Belousova, took their country's first figure-skating gold medals of many, and the ice hockey team began a domination that was to last until Lake Placid in 1980. The Swede, Sixten Jernberg, at thirty-five achieved gold medals in the 50-kilometres cross-country and relay for a total of four golds, three silvers and two bronzes in three Olympics.

Two died in the Games' preliminaries – a Polish-born British luger, Kay Skrzypecki, and an Australian skier, Ross Milne. More happily for Great Britain,

British gold: Tony Nash and Robin Dixon hurtle to the two-man bobsleigh gold at Innsbruck

the many times world bobsleigh champion, Eugenio Monti, ensured his own defeat and victory for Tony Nash and Robin Dixon when he rushed back a bolt from his own bob for the Britons to make an emergency repair before their final run. Even Brundage was forced to say at the closing ceremony, 'The Innsbruck Games have shown how much the human will is capable of achieving.'

X Grenoble 1968

Gaullist France introduced new elements of size, fashion and pride to the Winter Games. Screaming Mirages wrote five-ring smoke trails in the sky. Stereo sound eerily relayed the heartbeat of the skater Alain Calmat as he climbed the ninety-

Jean-Claude Killy's miserable 1968 season erupts: three gold medals at Grenoble to howls of Austrian protests that Karl Schranz won the slalom

six steps to ignite the Olympic flame, helicopters scattered 30,000 perfumed paper roses, and 300 French hostesses in red bunny fur and blue stretch pants set the caped and caparisoned teams more competition than they could handle in the field of looks and couture.

France, too, provided the principal hero of the Games. Jean-Claude Killy, like Sailer in 1956, took all three Alpine gold medals, though not without the kind of controversy which marked many aspects of these Games. Shortly before the start an Austrian girl filed a paternity suit which resulted in the Austrian police confiscating Killy's laundry at a Kitzbuehel hotel, an action which embarrassed as many Austrians as it infuriated the French. Then came accusations of professionalism, by Avery Brundage, directed against Nancy Greene of Canada as well as Killy.

Killy went into retreat for the Games, but emerged to win the downhill from fourteenth start place in spite of slushy snow. Gambling on a higher line in the traverse before the finish, he swooped in to take first place from his fellow countryman, Guy Perillat. Killy, with his lean, hawkish good looks, at twenty-four attracted a worldwide following. He next won the giant slalom, then – on the final day – the special slalom, but not without bitter protest from his oldest rival, Karl Schranz of Austria, a man gaining every ski-racing honour except an Olympic gold medal. Killy had a narrow lead on the first run, and appeared to have won on the aggregate of the two runs when Schranz was allowed a further run on the grounds that a policeman had crossed the track, distracting him. His time for the rerun would have given him the gold medal but the French now protested that Schranz could not have been distracted at gate 18 by anything happening at gate 21 – about 50 ft to 60 ft ahead – in bad visibility. The jury accepted the protest three to one with one abstention, to howls of protest from Schranz's supporters. Killy, garlanded with three gold medals, sold his picture to *Paris Match* for £3,000, signed with Mark McCormack, and became the first ski-racing millionaire. American skiers were challenged to beat him under a handicap system; Killy meantime endorsed anything from cameras to credit cards.

Brundage at Grenoble tried to ban the use of trade names on skis and other equipment, but national teams rebelled, aware that the ski circus needed a full-time commitment from the skiers and financial props from the ski industry to maintain championship levels of performance. A compromise was reached whereby skiers removed their equipment before being photographed or televised, but Brundage said wearily: 'It is reported that the French spent $240 million in connection with these Games and, when you consider this was for ten days of amateur sport, it seems to be somewhat out of proportion.' Sport, though, was no longer a simple pastime. Three East Germans were disqualified from the single-seater tobogganing for heating the runners of their sleds over an open fire in an effort to obtain greater speed. Skiers could use wax, tobogganists could not use fire under their federation rules.

More than half the Grenoble budget in fact went into permanent facilities such as motorways and housing. But Grenoble still prospered from some magnificent new sports facilities, including the indoor ice stadium, designed to seat 12,000 and available to the city for countless years ahead, unlike the bob run, built on a sunny slope at Alpe d'Huez, and impractical for further use in spite of the millions it cost. The bobbers had to rise well before dawn to use the ice before it melted. Eugenio Monti, at the age of forty, won both two- and four-man gold medals to go with his nine World Championships. The Protopopovs, at 35 and 32 respectively, again won the pairs skating. Franco Nones (Italy) won the 30 kilometres to become the first cross-country gold medallist from outside Scandinavia or the USSR. Grenoble, altogether, was an important crossroads in Olympic affairs.

The man who never skied the Sapporo Games: Karl Schranz came off the practice slopes to criticise Avery Brundage's 'obsolete ideas', then found himself expelled. He returned to Vienna an Austrian hero. The Olympics would never be the same again

XI Sapporo 1972

Sapporo, on the most northerly Japanese island of Hokkaido, lost the chance of the 1940 Winter Games because of the Second World War. Another war, one without gunshots, came to a head in 1972 when Avery Brundage, retiring as president of the IOC, expelled the world's best-known active ski-racer, Karl Schranz of Austria, on the eve of competition.

Schranz was the scapegoat of a bitter fight waged by Brundage to protect amateurism as he understood it. The 84-year-old American millionaire demanded in May 1971 that ten well-known skiers be disqualified from Games competition for coaching at a ski camp in California. The top six Alpine nations – Austria, France, Italy, Switzerland, West Germany and Yugoslavia – threatened to boycott the Sapporo Games if any skier was banned for professionalism. The FIS, whose president, Marc Hodler, was treasurer of the IOC, averted confrontation by condemning ski camps but pointed out that the skiers – who had received $50

The champion who lost: Bernhard Russi wins the Sapporo downhill gold but has to take second place to Klammer at Innsbruck in 1976

a day allowance – had obtained the permission of their national federations. Brundage maintained a determined personal opposition, producing a black list of fifty skiers whom he claimed were not eligible. His committee, aware of double standards, not least where state athletes were concerned, backed off an outright confrontation, but allowed Brundage to expel Schranz on the grounds of an interview given to Associated Press. In it he said, 'The Russians are subsidised by their own government and all international athletes get help from one source or another. It's an emphasis on the wrong principle. I think the Olympics should be a contest for all sportsmen, with no regard for colour, race or wealth.' Schranz was banned because he was 'the most blatant and the most verbose' that Brundage could find. His appeal to present his case to the IOC committee was dismissed by Brundage, who said, 'We don't deal with individuals.' It was an individual, not a group, who was punished, and the IOC was widely felt to have lost the moral argument.

The Games themselves, costing $555,556,000, or about £250 million, were saved. Schranz went home to a hero's reception in Vienna while appealing to his team to stay on. The Austrian tourist industry had invested in a superb Tyrolean chalet, which only emphasised the heavy commercial considerations of which

Asia's first Winter gold: Yukio Kasaya of Japan wins the 70-metre jump

Brundage complained. But the world at large wanted a winter festival, and the Japanese outlay of £121,000 on broadcasting facilities, and £365,000 on data-processing, was one more expression of that interest. Sapporo, which had grown from a sparse settlement to a city in less than a hundred years, believed its huge investment well worthwhile in establishing it as the principal ski city of the Orient.

Austrians tended to blame the Schranz affair for the failure of Annemarie Proell, the red-hot favourite for the women's downhill and giant slalom, to beat the 17-year-old Swiss, Marie-Therese Nadig, in either event. The victory of another Swiss, Bernhard Russi, in the men's downhill suggested an alternative explanation. At the crossroads of Siberian high- and Pacific low-pressure systems, the Sapporo mountains were subject to violent extremes of weather. The Swiss heavily researched snow types and conditions for the appropriate wax for their ski bases, and it undoubtedly contributed to their haul of six medals, including three golds, of the eighteen available. Gustavo Thoeni of Italy, four times overall World Cup winner in succeeding years, won the giant slalom, but the special slalom produced an outsider victory from Spain's Francisco Fernandez Ochoa. In the women's special slalom, Barbara Ann Cochran's victory was by the smallest ever margin – two hundredths of a second. Elsewhere, the Soviet Union collected eight medals from the cross-country, but the great surprise was the home success in ski jumping. Japan took all three medals in the 70-metres and won the jumping section of the combined. A Dutchman, Ard Schenk, became only the third speed skater to take three Olympic titles. Western journalists were intrigued by the romantic involvement between Aleksei Ulanov, partner of Irina Rodnina, and the second-ranking Russian pair skater, Ludmila Smirnova, partnering Andrei Suraikin on the ice. Rodnina and Ulanov won the pairs, in spite of the obvious coolness between them. Journalists writing 'From Russia with love' stories were loftily put down by Soviet coaches, but the famous Rodnina-Ulanov partnership was in fact dissolving and Ulanov later married Smirnova. Their partnership on the ice, though, met with little success.

An eventful Games of great sporting and social significance ended in chaos as the weather dumped a major blizzard on Sapporo. A few days earlier and competition would have been ruined.

XII Innsbruck 1976

Innsbruck's success saved the whole concept of the Winter Games. Lord Killanin, Avery Brundage's successor, warned that the twelfth Games could be the last unless Innsbruck proved that costs and commercialism could be controlled. He was not unaware that the IOC owed Austria some recompense after Brundage's treatment of Schranz. In the event, the quiet professionalism with which Innsbruck handled its second Games in twelve years entirely met the needs. Mayor Alois Lugger's team had only three years to prepare after Denver reneged on its agreement to hold the Games. Brundage would have exploited the Colorado referendum, which refused more funds to Denver, to bury the Winter Games. Killanin expressed the new liberalism. His own son had become a professional steeplechase jockey. Killanin nursed the new rule 26, which completely redefined eligibility, through the seventy-fifth IOC session at Vienna in October 1974. Athletes could be full-time, maintained, and with nest eggs set aside for their future, and still compete in Olympic Games. They could not carry advertisements like sandwich-board men. International federations were left to decide how to measure athletes' income. Effectively the IOC now recognised that the day of sport simply as a

Golden Rosi: West Germany's heroine of Innsbruck 76, Rosi Mittermaier, was champion runner-up until her double gold and a silver

pastime and recreation was finished. Between Sapporo and Innsbruck 1976, the movement had suffered the trauma of Munich and the attack of the Black September organisation. The IOC could not keep its head in the sand. As Baron de Coubertin once said, 'The Olympic movement has to be a part of the times in which it exists; it has to adapt to its environment.'

Innsbruck's thirty-seven events were watched by one and a half million spectators and 600 million televiewers, and scrupulous detailing of accounts showed that 230 million Austrian schillings (about $17 million) were spent in adding to, or modernising, Olympic sites plus costs for personnel and technical facilities. The overall cost was $44 million, with a planned deficit of about $4.5 million, a welcome cost-effectiveness after Grenoble and Sapporo. Austria began and ended the Games with a gold medal. The cry of the Austrian Chancellor, Bruno Kreisky, after Franz Klammer had won the downhill gold on the first day, belongs to posterity: 'You have saved the Games for Austria.'

No skier has ever faced greater pressure than Klammer, the 22-year-old farmer's son from Mooswald, on that first brilliant day on the Patscherkofel, Innsbruck's own mountain. Klammer went fifteenth, last of the top seed, with millions of his fellow countrymen living and dying with his juddering skis at their every twist and turn. He nearly missed a gate at the start, and at the interval trailed the 1972 champion, Bernhard Russi, by a formidable two-tenths of a second. As so often he made up time in the finish, cornering the Bear's Neck more daringly than any to sweep through the finish .13 of a second faster than Russi. Karl Schnabl descended on the last day like a swallow to win the 90-metre jumping in a spectacular climax, but betweentimes Austria had to give best to others. The Soviet Union and East Germany collected forty-six of the 111 medals, with the rest split among fourteen of the thirty-five competing countries.

West Germany's heroine was Rosi Mittermaier, born a few metres from the Austrian border, whose first-ever victory in downhill was followed by the special slalom, and set up hopes for a unique triple gold for a woman skier. Known to the ski world as the champion runner-up, Rosi Mittermaier was enjoying her new reputation, but at the last the golden gates jammed. Eighteen-year-old Kathy Kreiner of Canada put together a set of strong, stately turns to step up from ninth place – her best for the season – to take the GS gold, with Rosi runner-up. 'I didn't lose, I was beaten,' said Rosi with practised felicity. 'I'm sorry for her,' Kathy Kreiner offered, 'but I'm much more pleased for me.'

East Germany captured both bob titles, and two of the three events involving jumping. A country without a serious mountain had never achieved as much in a Winter Games. The East Germans' refrigerated bob run and plastic slopes served them well. John Curry of Britain won the men's figure skating in spite of widely-quoted criticism of judges who downmarked his balletic style as not being sufficiently masculine, but Curry disciplined his approach and every necessary athletic element was in his programme. Irina Rodnina retained her pair title with her new partner Alexander Zaitsev. Ludmila Pachomova and Alexander Garschkov of the Soviet Union won the first-ever gold medal in ice dancing.

XIII Lake Placid 1980

Such are the organisational problems of a modern Winter Olympics that the IOC now decides on a venue six years in advance. In 1974 at Vienna, Lake Placid was the only bidder. It was the second time around, as it was for St Moritz and Innsbruck earlier, but between 1932 and 1980 the Olympics had mushroomed into a worldwide spectacle. In 1932 a budget of just over a million dollars could enable a community of 2,930 souls to stage a festival amid the Adirondack woods, lakes and mountains for 330 winter sportsmen from seventeen nations. This time the Olympic community had swelled to 6,000 athletes, officials and media. Now there were eight sports, with Alpine skiing, biathlon and tobogganing to go with the speed and figure skating, ice hockey, Nordic skiing and bobsleigh. The 'North Country Boys', headed by the Reverend J. Bernard Fell, still thought the village ideal a valid one. The offer was as desperate as the IOC's acceptance. The community was dying, its population down to 2,731. In the event the community bankrupted itself and only the intervention of New York State and the federal authorities kept the Games going.

Invincibility on ice: Irina Rodnina and Alexander Zaitsev of the Soviet Union win their second and her third pair skating gold at Lake Placid

A Games totally dependent on public transport within a proscribed no-car zone suffered a near-total breakdown of the bus system. At one point the system depended on one telephone, with only thirty of the necessary 300 buses operational. Thousands had to foot it from car parks five miles and more from sites, some in sneaker shoes or light car jackets. Many from Albany, New York and other metropolitan centres had no conception of the ferocity of wilderness winters; in the Nordic pre-Olympics a year before temperatures sank to minus 30°C. Providence intervened and only the women's downhill was hit by that sort of weather.

America has lift-off: Eric Heiden's space-age image dominated the Lake Placid ice with five speed-skating gold medals

Governor Hugh Carey of New York warned that people could better watch the Games on television in the comfort of their sitting-rooms. Five hundred million followed his advice.

The Games quickly established a pattern. Everything on the ice or snow worked well. Everything off it did not. Marc Hodler, president of the FIS, summed it up: 'Lake Placid proved that it is better to run the Alpine skiing on man-made snow than the real thing.' A few athletes demurred at staying in a prison – the Village was due to become a penitentiary after the Games. In truth, the architecture resembled many a modern university. The problem, as the Reverend Fell saw it, was the spectators. 'Maybe it's time to ban them,' he was reported as saying.

The Americans who gutsily made it were rewarded with triumph as well as

Liechtenstein fairy-tale: German-born Hanni Wenzel matched Rosi Mittermaier with two golds and a silver in the 1980 Alpine skiing

travesty. The US Olympic ice hockey team, hyped by Herb Brooks, buoyed up by a nation deep into the hostages in Iran, Afghanistan and the potential Moscow boycott, beat the Russians 4–3, and 'The Star Spangled Banner' echoed around America. Brooks's aphorisms became a part of American legend. 'Gentlemen, you don't have enough talent to win on talent alone.' The team came together for one campaign, then split up for good. Finland was beaten 4–2 in a final which verged on the anticlimactic. Eric Heiden was America's individual golden boy. While Mike Eruzione's winner against the Russians froze a moment of team ecstasy nine minutes into the final period, Heiden's 29-inch thighs, so developed that they affected his walk, pumped to and fro, day after day, in almost mind-boggling repetition as he won the 500, 1,000, 1,500, 5,000 and finally the 10,000 metres on the 400-metre speed-skating track. No one had ever won all five races before, and Heiden, to the USA, was now to ice what Mark Spitz was to chlorinated water.

East Germany, second only to the USSR in the 1976 medal count, now overhauled her neighbour with twenty-three medals based on a programme of systematised state sport. Anett Poetzsch took the women's figure skating and Jan Hoffman, with the performance of his life, pushed the favourite, Britain's Robin Cousins, to the very limits. A British television audience estimated at four million stayed up until the small hours to see Cousins stave off Hoffman's challenge. Rodnina and Zaitsev retained the pairs. Meinhard Nehmer, another of the GDR's stars, in winning the four-man bob added a third gold to his impressive record, and a fellow-countryman, Ulrich Wehling, took his third gold in successive Olympics in the combined 15-kilometre cross-country and 70-metre jumping.

On Whiteface's man-made snow, Austria again captured the downhills. Klammer, surprisingly, was dropped, but Leonhard Stock – originally a reserve – came through to take the men's and Annemarie Moser-Proell, who missed Innsbruck and was runner-up in Sapporo, gained her first Olympic gold. The greatest woman skier of her decade was, at twenty-six, winning her thirty-fourth downhill in sixty-four races. In eleven others she had come second or third, and this despite a twenty-month temporary retirement. Even so, the major female Alpine star was Liechtenstein's Hanni Wenzel, runner-up to Proell, but a winner, like Rosi Mittermaier, of two golds and a silver, the golds coming in the giant and special slaloms. Ingemar Stenmark of Sweden likewise won the giant and special slaloms for his first Olympic gold medals.

On the last major day Nikolai Zimyatov won his third and Russia's sixth Nordic gold medal. Lord Killanin warned of the holocaust while speaking with feeling of the contribution sport made to understanding between nations. His efforts to stop an American boycott of the Moscow Olympics had been in vain. In the Indian Ocean, two Soviet fighters venturing too close to the US aircraft carrier, *Coral Sea*, were intercepted by an American fighter. The Russians suddenly broke radio silence: 'Congratulations on your ice-hockey victory,' the voice said in English.

4
RECROWNING OF THE KAISER

For three years Franz Klammer travelled the world ski circuit an emperor in exile, a monarch like Haile Selassie of Ethiopia, or Zog of Albania, who never would return to his long-ago land. Still offered the eminence and protocol of former office; still applauded respectfully for results in the top twenty; listened to with genuine sorrow and respect after unsought indignities; being dropped, for instance, from the Austrian Olympic team at Lake Placid and plunging that season to thirty-third in the downhill rankings.

People wanted to remember him for Innsbruck 1976, for his 1:45.3 seconds of all-out attack on the two-mile Patscherkofel, a golden run to satisfy the double eagle of Austria's skiing pride. Klammer, like a young winged god, restored not only Austria – still seething after the expulsion of Karl Schranz from Sapporo – but the concept of athletic heroism and simple dignity. He could win with a smile. And as the world came to know, he could lose with a smile. If ever an athlete conformed to Baron de Coubertin's ideal of the taking part being more important than the winning then it was the Carinthian farm boy.

Klammer, born 3 December 1953 in the little town of Mooswald, hard by the Yugoslav border of southern Austria, was twenty years old when he won his first downhill on the fast and treacherous course of Schladming, fifty miles south of Salzburg in the province of Styria, in 1973. Schladming is the home of Charlie Kahr, 'Downhill Charlie' of the Austrian men's team, a wispy little man with lugubrious grey-blue eyes who was soon to begin his long, still unbroken reign as the guru of the Austrian men's downhill team. A downhiller for Charlie must have intelligence of the feet, an instinct for gliding, strength, athletic ability and an uncomplicated approach. He must be confident, even arrogant. 'He must have guts and he must have a nervousness before he starts – the right kind of nervousness. He must also be hungry for success and recognition, and it does not matter if he is born poor. Klammer has the strength of generations, but he was born poor. It did him no harm. He had something to prove on the mountains.'

In 1974–5 Klammer won eight of nine downhills – Val d'Isère, St Moritz,

The race he had to win: Franz Klammer takes the Olympic downhill gold at Innsbruck, 1976

Kitzbuehel, Wengen, Garmisch, Val Gardena, Innsbruck and Jackson Hole, each in record time. At Wengen it was by the World Cup record-breaking margin of 3.54 seconds. The beaky-nosed 21-year-old with the ready smile and clean-cut approach to life had inherited not just an Austrian but a world domain. 'He took more chances,' said Kahr. 'He held his tuck where others were jerked upright. He set new limits.' Klammer also had the advantage of the most advanced downhill ski available. The Fischer ski company has as its emblem three triangles. They represent design, organisation and technique. Deep in the Bohemian countryside north-east of Salzburg, at the company town of Ried-im-Incress, where the hours are conditioned to the workers feeding their animals at dawn and dusk, sophisticated minds had worked on a ski test-bed.

The ski is not a simple object. It is the product of an advanced, computerised industry that must relate geometric form to the properties of wood, metals, alloys and plastics. Klammer, on the Fischer experimental track at Tauplitz, was a test pilot. Johann Stroi, in charge of racing experimentation, would check and measure skis, base waxes, boots, suits, helmets, sticks, techniques of sliding, turning, traversing, carving, straight running. Transmitters on the two-kilometre course automatically registered Klammer's speed and edging control in different temperatures and moisture levels of snow. A read-out on a magnetic tape showed the exact distribution of force on the soles of Klammer's feet. The testing became ever more sophisticated. Small lights built into Klammer's boots showed when he was edging left or right. 'He didn't know himself when he was edging. The lights helped,' said Stroi. 'He was a bad slider when he was young – the first two years. With the help of the lights he became much better.'

In 1976 Klammer was again the World Cup downhill title-holder, winning Kitzbuehel, Wengen, Morzine, Aspen and Madonna di Campiglio. And, in the midst of it, the Olympic title. The argument raged among purists. Who was the greatest skier of his time, Klammer or the Swedish slalom wizard, Ingemar Stenmark? Both were specialists, but to Austrians the answer was clear. 'You can lose any race in Austria except one – the downhill,' Kahr said. Jackie Stewart, no stranger to high-speed pressures, watched Klammer's Innsbruck run from the ABC television commentary box. 'No one has ever won a race under more pressure,' he said. Through it all Klammer kept his balance and charm.

Klammer from a distance seemed the playboy – good looking, coolly playing the publicity game dreamed up by his ski-makers and others, a string of lovely girls in his wake. At closer range it was the strength of mind which compelled. He remained the mountain farmer's son who grew up with the seasons, learning early to assess real values. 'What Stenmark has done in two disciplines which are hazardous as well as technical is prodigious. He has to pay a price, though, and to me it is his solitude.' Or this. 'My life is marvellous. I adore the speed, the turns which I am trying to take ever more quickly, to transmit to my skis what I have done in my head. Skiing for me is a hobby, and what is more marvellous than to do the things one loves?'

The Olympic season was followed in 1976–7 by another year of World Cup triumph – Val d'Isère twice, Garmisch, Kitzbuehel, Wengen, Laax all won. In the following season rumours were floated in the Austrian press, which ran a Klammer story almost every day, that he would consider a professional offer after the 1978 World Championships in Garmisch-Partenkirchen. At Val d'Isère for the start of the 1978–9 season there was little sign of tension, but an offer to turn pro for one million dollars over four seasons had been made. If he was to take it up, every race now was crucial. The statistics of Klammer's career were amazing – forty races, twenty-one victories, twice thirteenth, once eleventh, and every other time in the first five in completed races. He knew at Val d'Isère that he had to re-establish his supremacy after a final race the season before of relative disaster – eleventh place at Heavenly Valley, USA, to an Austrian 'unknown', Bartl Gensbichler.

Val d'Isère's two major hazards, the Collombin Jump and the Compression, are by-words of downhill skiing. If weakness existed with Klammer it was supposed to be his jumping. The technique at the time was the pre-jump, an anticipatory flexing just before the crest of a bump which reduced time in the air. Klammer had eliminated the pre-jump four years earlier when the technique failed him at Chamonix and he suffered one of his few falls, hurting his head and shoulder. 'I decided never again, and I would stay crouched trying to swallow a bump.' It was to be a technique almost universally adopted in later seasons, as speeds increased and the positive motion of pre-jumping became seriously dangerous if even slightly misjudged. Klammer on the Collombin of Val d'Isère this time flew forty metres where others had kept it to thirty. 'Maybe I have lost tenths of a second here and there and afterwards I hear five are faster at the intermediate stage, just like the Olympics. Then I come to the Compression, which is the most important part of all. It is where your speed is high and you must hit this uphill part and turn almost at the same time. You must be fast into the Compression and even faster out. The way you leave decides the race . . . I come out smiling to myself. I love bumps and compressions. These are what I do best.' It was victory again for Klammer and this time an English language interview. Two years before Klammer could scarcely say, 'Good morning.' Now, sitting in the comfortable lounge of the three-star Savoyarde, Gery Krims, the Fischer racing manager, brings champagne. 'It's good champagne,' he says. 'Good enough for us,' says Klammer, laughing. It is only five years since his first victory bought his father his first milking machine.

Suddenly the champagne was flat and the milk sour. Klammer's hopes of a million-dollar coup melted in the soft snow and dank air of the Zugspitze, West Germany's highest mountain, above Garmisch-Partenkirchen. The World Championship which Klammer had needed to win belonged once again to Austria, but in the keeping of Sepp Walcher, who was content enough with a three-foot Bavarian wood carving of a skier and a gold-plated medal. Klammer, a disconsolate fifth, went off to ski in solitude in Carinthia. Krims was asked to stand down by Fischer because he had grown too close to Klammer. It was a major shock for the circuit. Krims, with a budget of £700,000 a year and fifteen servicemen, only three of whom serviced the Austrian team, had helped make his company's name all over the world. Klammer won Laax to finish first in the World Cup downhill standings for the fourth successive year. It was his last victory until Val d'Isère in December 1981, nearly four years later.

Klammer gave up all hopes of a professional career. The American professional

Fire and fury: Klammer sets out on the comeback trail with a new ski

circuit was geared to parallel slalom, an easier, less expensive set-piece for the commercial TV cameras. He also switched skis, from the ash-core Fischer to the foam-core Kneissl. They never seemed to suit him, but under the rules of the Austrian team's equipment-pool arrangements racers are strictly debarred from voicing public criticisms. Some put his decline down to the downhill accident to his 16-year-old brother Klaus, who was left paralysed from the waist down. Klammer jibbed at that theory. 'You cannot race with fear. Nervousness, yes.' In 1979 he finished nineteenth in the World Cup downhill rankings, and in 1980 he was not only dropped from the Olympic four at Lake Placid but finished only eleventh in World Cup. 'I lost my pleasure in skiing. I wanted to leave the mountain and swim in the lake.' A switch back to a wood-core ski, Blizzard, revived his spirits, but in 1980–1 he could still manage no better than thirteenth, with his best result sixth at Cortina. Most still thought that, like many veteran Grand Prix drivers, Klammer was aiming slightly off, content with the autumnal blooms. How wrong they were.

Klammer married a blonde Viennese medical student from a distinctly middle-class background, and the security of the relationship clearly meant much to him. A change of boot and the consolidation of his test work with Blizzard brought him fresh and eager to the 1981–2 season. On 6 December 1981 Val d'Isère witnessed the outstanding downhill comeback of modern times. Three days after his twenty-eighth birthday, all that driving leg power, intuition and glide-feel powered him

New challenger (*above*): Conradin Cathomen, with victories at Val Gardena 1 and Val d'Isère 2, pressed Klammer to the last. *Opposite*: Austrian thrust: Erwin Resch joined Klammer and Harti Weirather in a major push for the title

down the Oreiller-Killy piste in 2:5.22. The king could not be said to be back on his throne after one victory, but second at Kitzbuehel and fourth at Wengen kindled hopes for the World Championship at Schladming. A fall on the final day's training in ruts left by competitors in the heavily criticised combined wrecked Klammer's chances. Black and blue, he still managed seventh place behind Harti Weirather, a performance a crowd of 60,000 cheered. The course which eight years before had witnessed his first victory was still a favourite with Klammer, and he was still an idol in Austria. He saw out the season quietly, with only twelfth place at Aspen to show for his three North American downhills, but overall he finished respectably in fifth place, his 71 points comparing with Steve Podborski's winning 115. North American snow and courses have not always suited Klammer's style: Whistler is too flat, Aspen too dependent on the glide at the top. The 'Klammer Express' likes to smoke late and hard on courses such as Kitzbuehel, Wengen and Val d'Isère, whose key sections rise in crescendo.

Klammer began his tenth season with an appetite totally renewed. 'Now I think once again what I can win by, not by how much I lose.' He was aware how

ellesse
11

Jet start (*above*): Klammer was second, third and first in the opening three races, but doubted he could maintain it. *Below*: Disaster at Sarajevo: Ex-champion Peter Mueller, having won the first Super G, crashed badly on the Olympic downhill course

False dawn: Harti Weirather won the first race at Pontresina but could not follow it up

things had changed since the 1970s. 'Then there were just one or two to beat, now there are so many. Austria has a very good base of downhillers. Then there are the Swiss and Canadians. The differences are very small.' The season's pattern of weather and travel disruption was quickly established, with the first race switched to Pontresina because of the lack of snow at Laax, but on an unfamiliar course Klammer was twenty points to the good in second place to Weirather. Val d'Isère for the fifth year suffered miserable weather, but the switch to Val Gardena in the Dolomites did Klammer no harm. Where Steve Podborski slumped to twenty-fourth place, to follow his mediocre twelfth at Pontresina, Klammer was third to Switzerland's Conradin Cathomen, the World Championship silver medallist. Cathomen, 23, was 108th in the FIS rankings two years earlier. After changing skis three times he had finally made it to the top. Next day it was Klammer's turn. Second down, he had a tantalising wait as racer after racer attacked his time of

'Golf Sieger': Canada's Todd Brooker, six handicap golfer, won Kitzbuehel's Hahnenkamm and Aspen

2:8.91. Switzerland's Peter Mueller, who lost the title to Podborski only on a count-back, had a better intermediate time but lost ground on the lower turns.

Austria not only celebrated another Klammer victory but began to speculate whether he could keep it going. Podborski had clearly been set back by a summer of promotional activities. Canada's Ken Read, another veteran, was skiing well, but not quite well enough to win. When victory could obviously go to any in the top twenty, those holing the early putts were clearly going to steal an advantage. Britain's Konrad Bartelski, so rightly proud of his top-fifteen seeding, suffered cruel luck at Val Gardena, the course where he achieved his second place the previous year. Free skiing before the first race he fell on a tree stump. Badly bruised, he missed both races and never again gathered momentum.

With Morzine cancelled, Val d'Isère picked up the pass for two downhills in successive days. Erwin Resch of Austria won the first and Cathomen the second, to lead the downhill standings by 9 points from Klammer. With the racers able to count their best five results there was still much to play for. Even Podborski, in spite of his bad start, could make a bid with six races left. Wengen gloomily gave up its classic to Kitzbuehel, belated snow falling so heavily and threateningly that every ski lift in the Bernese Oberland was closed because of avalanche danger. Kitzbuehel's week began much the same, but suddenly the clouds parted, the sun shone, and in a glittering two days the downhill circuit's spirits were restored.

Bump champ: Gerhard 'Pfaffy' Pfaffenbichler mastered Sarajevo's bumps for his first World Cup victory

Bruno Kernen, a 21-year-old from the Swiss third team, came from twenty-ninth place to win the first race, the translated Lauberhorn, thus denying the second-placed Podborski, at last showing title-holding form. Klammer had his worst run of the season to finish forty-third, but in the Hahnenkamm proper the following day he bounced back into sixth place behind Todd Brooker of Canada, the fifth different winner of the season.

Brooker, 23, from Paris, Ontario, once again cost Rick Gunnell, English owner of The Londoner pub in Kitzbuehel, a couple of hundred bottles of champagne as Canada and the English-speaking racing community revelled through much of the night. It was Canada's fourth successive Hahnenkamm, but Brooker was only the fourth Canadian to win a World Cup event. Austrian newspapers lamented their team's failure, bemoaning skis, training, self-confidence, leadership – everything short of the *apfelstrudel*. Desperate to reclaim some Austrian aspect, one newspaper described the freckled, sandy-haired Brooker as Canada's Klammer. Brooker's second place at Aspen the previous winter had been a forewarning. Remarkably, he cannot run, swim or play soccer – all conventional downhill training activities – because of a knee which has undergone seven operations and looks as lumpy as a mangold. But he compensates well enough with weight training and roller skating, and when he disclosed a golf handicap of six a German newspaper was quick to dub him the '*Golf Sieger*', or golf champion.

Second-seed victory: Switzerland's Bruno Kernen came from 29th to win Wengen's Lauberhorn trophy at Kitzbuehel

It was a first victory with consequences, for Brooker joined the considerable batting order of men with a chance of the World Cup title. Podborski kept his form going with second place behind the Austrian outsider, Gerhard Pfaffenbichler, at Sarajevo. The joky nature of the start, with the skiers whistling off a start house perched on a restaurant roof, was scarcely matched by an unjoky finish on the course that was being tried out for the next season's Olympics. Klammer admitted to backing off the final bump, which he described tersely as too dangerous, but still made third place. The day of the race brought few falls, in the event, but a horrific looking somersault by Mueller in the last day's training caused concussion and the loss of two races which effectively finished his bid for a third World Cup downhill title.

The final European downhill, the St Anton Arlberg-Kandahar, helped prove little except the courage and persistence of Switzerland's Peter Luescher, the most derided of World Cup winners. In 1979 Luescher took the overall title while winning only one race, a slalom, and never scoring a point in downhill, though that year the top twenty-five were awarded points. Now, at twenty-six, after a knee operation, he skied faster and more positively than at any time in his life to

Late starter: Steve Podborski, 1982 title-holder, set back by a summer of promotional activities

win his first downhill, followed at Garmisch by a Super Giant Slalom, so that he briefly led the overall standings. No one begrudged success to a remarkably game performer, but it left everything to play for in North America, where Aspen and Lake Louise staged the last two downhills.

Aspen proved a bitter-sweet experience for Canada. A major row rocked the team when the Canadian Ski Association, in grave financial difficulties, demanded $2,065 (£1,150) from all 'A' team members, Podborski, the World Cup downhill title-holder, included. Head coach John Ritchie, the man who had led them to their downhill eminence, showed his feelings on the matter by prematurely announcing his retirement and describing the demand as outrageous. With Podborski, Read and Brooker among eight skiers who could take the current title, the announcement could not have come at a more damaging time for morale. On the same day, ironically, the Canadian government announced a grant of $25 million to winter-oriented sports for training and coaching up to the 1988 Winter Games in Calgary. Todd Brooker pointed out that while top skiers did make individual contracts with ski manufacturers, twenty-five per cent of their earnings went to the Association. Robin McLeish, a young married man in the A team, said quite candidly that his trust fund would not cover the levy and he could not pay it. Brooker went straight out and won the race, which left Canada with a fantastic climax on the home snow of Lake Louise on 12 March, even though Podborski fell, injuring a knee ligament badly enough to kill his chances, if not, as was at one time feared, his career.

The World Cup has seen a number of close downhill finishes, but none as close as this one, as a table prepared on the eve of the race showed:

WORLD CUP POINTS RACE

	Points	Best five 1982-83 and points awarded					Possibilities at Lake Louise		
							MPP	MTP	FReq
1 Klammer	86	1st 25	2nd 20	3rd 15	3rd 15	5th 11	14	100	4th
2 Cathomen	85	1st 25	1st 25	3rd 15	4th 12	8th 8	17	102	7th
3 Weirather	74	1st 25	3rd 15	4th 12	5th 11	5th 11	14	88	4th
4 Luescher	72	1st 25	2nd 20	6th 10	7th 9	8th 8	17	89	7th
Raeber	72	2nd 20	3rd 15	3rd 15	4th 12	6th 10	15	87	5th
6 Mueller	71	2nd 20	3rd 15	4th 12	4th 12	4th 12	13	84*	3rd
7 Read	69	2nd 20	3rd 15	4th 12	5th 11	5th 11	14	83*	4th
8 Brooker	67	1st 25	1st 25	6th 10	11th 5	14th 2	23	90	13th
9 Resch	64	1st 25	2nd 20	5th 11	11th 5	13th 3	22	86	12th
10 Podborski	63	2nd 20	2nd 20	4th 12	9th 7	12th 4	21	84*	11th

Points Current World Cup downhill points after 10 races
MPP Maximum points possible for a win at Lake Louise. That is, 25 points for the win minus those points counting for a racer's current fifth-best result
MTP Maximum total points a racer will be counting following a win at Lake Louise
FReq Finish required at Lake Louise for minimal improvement in a racer's point total
* Cannot win overall title

Seven men could now win. Klammer and Cathomen were joint favourites, but Brooker could overthrow them from eighth place if he won and the two Europeans failed to finish in the first three. Brooker went fifth, Cathomen twelfth and Klammer fifteenth. The sky above the regal Rocky peaks of the Banff National Park was deep blue. At last a day to mark a great downhill occasion. Brooker's first interval time was fastest of all the first seed, as the subsequent timing showed. So was the second interval. Through 'Double Trouble', where two big bumps spell disaster for the slightest mistake at 80 mph, Brooker stayed fastest. But on the final knoll before the finish, a tenth of a second faster than any, Brooker's long legs suddenly convulsed, checked, spread and spun. Canada groaned.

Now, so quick the action, climax succeeding climax, Cathomen was over the knoll and finishing fastest in 1:40.77. The mind had scarcely gobbled that up when Klammer's first interval-time boomed — 39.55, slower than Brooker and Cathomen, but not much. Over the final crest, now, that crouched cannon-ball of silken white and blue stripe. The flashing scoreboard stopped its winking as

The loser winneth (*above*): Peter Luescher, 1979 World Cup title-holder and never an individual win, triumphed in the St Anton downhill and Garmisch Super G. *Below*: Austrian start: Helmut Hoeflehner, the practice champion, won well at Lake Louise

thousands of minds groped for the implications. The glossy-suited Austrian racers in the finish area were quickest to grasp the story. Leaping, shouting, exultant, keen foes of a few moments before, they tore over to Klammer to hoist him on their shoulders and slap on a cowboy stetson. Klammer had beaten Cathomen by two hundredths of a second. The Kaiser was truly king again, a

Power to the Swiss: Urs Raeber joined Mueller, Cathomen and Luescher among Switzerland's contenders

season's work, nearly four years of frustration, resolved by a margin equivalent to the blink of a camera shutter, or two and a half feet at the 80 mph at which downhillers finish a course.

The fact that another Austrian, the second-seeded Helmut Hoeflehner, came in with 1:40.52 for first place was barely anticlimax. Klammer kept repeating, 'The race is not yet over.' He could not afford to be pushed into fourth place. Top sportsmen know exactly what is possible from any situation, both for themselves and for others. Klammer, when all danger was past, could relax and enjoy himself, but he was still completely objective. Innsbruck in 1976, he said, was much more pressure. 'I had to win.' It was perfectly possible to continue after thirty, but you

Canadian disappointment: Todd Brooker, latest of the Crazy Canucks, crashed at Lake Louise with the title in his grasp

had to like the travelling and pressure. 'It is always more difficult in front of your home crowd. It is the first time Todd Brooker has experienced it.' Klammer had skied well in December, but after his fifth place at Val d'Isère he had thought, 'Kaput'. 'I never thought I could keep it going with so many able to win. This is the best I have ever skied in North America. Seven could have won going into the last race. Never, I think, has it been so close or won by so few points. I made it and I am very happy.'

The most disrupted season since the World Cup began in 1967 had seen nine different winners. It bore out Klammer's general point. Better fitness and materials, plus increasing sophistication in training techniques, had left victories by

Hero in a stetson: Klammer congratulates Hoeflehner. Cathomen misses out by .02 of a second

his 1975 margins in the ski archives. The king was no longer a Hapsburg but a Juan Carlos. All the same, he shows little signs of slowing down. 'As long as I enjoy it I will continue, certainly in 1984 and maybe after that.'

More sadly, downhill said farewell to Ken Read, who opened the door for Podborski, Irwin and Brooker with his Val d'Isère victory in 1975, and Konrad Bartelski, 'the crazy Brit', as the *Calgary Herald* dubbed him. 'In reality there is neither a British ski team nor a national coach,' the paper said. 'Konrad Bartelski was both.' Europeans were certainly amazed that a country without mountains, as they perceived it, should have a first-seed downhiller. They overlooked that both Podborski and Brooker came from regions of Ontario where the hills are about the same elevation as Hampstead Heath in London, and that Scotland, north of Glasgow and Edinburgh, is pretty well all mountain, but that is where another generation has risen to follow Bartelski. The Briton had a poor season compounded by worries over back-up which cost him essential concentration, problems with his skis, and the profound ill-luck of missing Val Gardena because of a training injury. Aspen finally convinced him he must give up. 'I was repeatedly in the top three in the first part of the course in training, but my finish in the race was a joke – fourth from last.' Like Read, Bartelski saw no challenge in the Sarajevo Olympic course, and with an opportunity to help in ski-related business, he decided to

Ken Read (*left*): first of the Crazymen but time now to quit. Konrad Bartelski (*right*): his last race was Lake Louise. The Sarajevo course is not for him

quit. 'I wanted to stay close to skiing and put something back. Martin Bell has shown that when things go his way he doesn't let the chance slip, which we haven't seen for some time.'

Bell's twenty-fourth at Aspen, from a start position of fifty-five, was Britain's best result of the season. 'If I've done nothing else, I think my career has taught that it is possible for a Briton, or for any small country, to go out and win World Cup, beating the Austrians and the rest of the Alpine countries,' said Bartelski. 'But you have to have dedication and leadership. In leadership we still have some way to go. We could also do with more pooled resources among the smaller countries, but nationalism interferes.' Bartelski, besides his second at Val Gardena in World Cup, was fifteenth in the 1974 World Championships and twelfth at the Lake Placid Olympics, a record which Bell now hopes to surpass.

Bell, 19, is the first of a new breed of young Scot with a snow background from early days. A concentrated, ambitious racer, able to pass A levels at fifteen and submerge himself in the German-speaking environment of the Austrian Ski Academy at Stams, near Innsbruck, he lost all the 1981–2 season through a knee injury caused by an accident at the academy when he stumbled on a loose floorboard in the dark. He also missed five World Cup races in 1982–3 because of a training fall, in which he dislocated an elbow, at the British Championships at

Val d'Isère. Aspen gave him 17.72 handicap points. He was little more than three seconds behind the winner, Todd Brooker, and beat Olympic champion Leonhard Stock and silver medallist Peter Wirnsberger. The Kandahar club and others supported him and his equally promising brother Graham in New Zealand races in the summer of 1983, Graham qualifying for World Cup downhill with his results. Martin suffered the further setback of strained ligaments, in the other knee this time, when he caught an edge and fell in the first race. Once again he lost precious summer training time, but he could still be optimistic for the team. 'We have a group now aged from seventeen to nineteen who can be really competitive with each other and raise the whole level of performance,' he said. 'We've a lot to look forward to.' Bartelski by his example, and Klammer by the huge television public he drew in Britain as elsewhere, helped to create that opportunity.

It was a major disappointment, then, when the British Ski Federation in October announced itself so short of funds that the women's team of six could no longer be supported. The British Sports Council joined in the outcry, wanting to know how its Alpine grant of £73,000 was being spent. The Federation reallocated funds and reinstated the women's trainer and programme. At the same time the FIS threatened to remove all World Cup races from France with French television announcing it had insufficient funds to cover them. The White Circus was all set for another season of tumbling acts and derring-do.

5

A MAHRE WITH A MISSION

When you sit down to talk ski with Phil Mahre you see a life stripped to its essentials. 'No American ski racer had ever won a World Cup until Phil Mahre won three,' *Time* magazine said of him. In the same week Tamara McKinney from Lexington, Kentucky, sewed up the women's World Cup overall. America's skiing bloodstock had suddenly developed a pedigree to rival the blue-grass country.

Mahre saw it without romanticism. We sat in a Lake Louise hotel, the World Cup overall won, reviewing his season. His thoughts were on World Cup politics, on the razzmatazz of the circuit, on life in Europe with a baby on his knee, and where it was all leading. Mahre had not won a race until the Aspen giant slalom on 7 March. Then he won Vail, USA, and Furano, Japan, with a late-season burst which carried him 67 points ahead of Sweden's Ingemar Stenmark, and 108 better than third-placed Andreas Wenzel of Liechtenstein, both World Cup winners of earlier years. 'I just wasn't as intense or nearly as concentrated as I have been in the past,' he said. 'I could barely put two runs together, and that was just lack of concentration. I just wasn't tough and mentally prepared as I was last year. I've a family now, and there's a lot more important things in life than ski-racing, and it carries over into my results, I think.'

That may seem strange to hear from only the third man, after Gustavo Thoeni and Ingemar Stenmark, to win the World Cup three times, but not to those who have followed the contained, sometimes insular, careers of the Mahre twins over the years. Steve, four minutes the junior and always trying to catch up, has been Phil's closest friend and rival since they hit the circuit in 1976, with Phil overall fourteenth and Steve twenty-seventh. Phil could exult in his brother's biggest win, the World Championship giant slalom in 1982, yet say, 'I had a twin brother who pushed me in the sense that I always wanted to beat him. Yet at the same time his victories were sort of my victories too.' They had a father, Dave, who learned about Phil's second World Cup triumph while he was roping up Everest. Dave, mountain manager of the White Pass ski area of the Cascade mountains in Washington state, gave them a pair of skis and a simple philosophy to cope with

En famille: Phil Mahre toured Europe with his 20-year-old wife Holly and infant daughter Lindsay. Steve Mahre also took his family

success. The Mahres, paradoxically, are more European than North American heroes. At Kennedy airport in 1982–3 they were simply two lookalike guys with thinning hair, smoked glasses, babes slung over their shoulders, keeping an eye on stickered bags with planks and poles. It wasn't a classic fan situation, in spite of *Time* and a couple of stories in *Sports Illustrated*, though slowly the television exposure of World Cup skiing is growing in the USA.

Travelling en famille – Phil with Holly, his 20-year-old wife, and five-month-old daughter Lindsay; Steve with Debbie, 21, and fifteen-month-old daughter Ginger – was an attempt to overcome the to-and-fro miseries of the European ski circuit. Phil considers some of these miseries are avoidable. 'The Europeans dominate the sport. People who make the schedule are people who don't race. They can get up at 10.30 and finish writing about it at 3.30 and be on their way. The racers get up at 6 am to train and race, when they've not reached their hotels until 1 am. We travel across Europe several times from west to east, then east back to west, and we make nine-hour drives two or three times a week. That's ridiculous. We are too much in the hands of people who want to sponsor. We're up and down Europe like a yo-yo, especially, like this year, when there's no snow and the schedule is being jockeyed around every week, or every other day. The Europeans can go home. We can't.'

The racers put their case to FIS president Marc Hodler after the 1982 finals.

Downhill pay-off: Phil Mahre skied his best downhill campaign to pick up priceless points

'I pointed out that we wouldn't get home after Christmas until late March,' said Mahre. 'That's three months on the move. Nobody should have to do that. Okay, they said, we see the point, but they turn around and do it wrongly anyway. If they don't listen to the racers, why should they listen to officials?'

The 1982–3 season was hard on top racers for reasons other than scheduling. Bill Marolt, the US team director, said, 'The whole US team let down after Phil's runaway and Steve winning the World Championship GS. Everyone was shooting at us, but everyone had bad summer and autumn snow so the quality wasn't there. Even Stenmark failed to finish races.' The Swiss were more consistent after southern hemisphere training and racing. They also made a dead set at the newly-introduced single-run Super Giant Slalom, a hybrid between downhill and the shorter, two-run giant slalom which, over the years, course-setters had begun to set more like a slalom with shorter, sharper turns. FIS aimed to encourage downhillers to try for Super G points and thus improve their chances in the overall. Mahre refused categorically to race it, much reducing his points potential in GS since the Super comprised three of the ten races from which he could count his five best under World Cup rules.

'They forced an event on us and they don't know what it stands for,' said Mahre. 'At the racers' meeting with FIS I voiced my opinion that this event was supposedly for downhillers and yet they scored it as a giant slalom. They really

Difficult year: Steve Mahre, fourth at Courmayeur, won the Parpan and St Anton slaloms but suffered injury problems

don't know what they're doing. You talk to anyone on the circuit. Nobody agrees with it, but nobody's going to say "no". It's up to the World Cup committee, where Serge Lang [the chairman] has the final say and everyone has to agree. They all said I couldn't win the World Cup if I did no Super G and I've won the World Cup. I've done things my way and I've done it without Super G. It's detrimental to the sport and I won't participate in it or promote something I don't believe in.'

Mahre could have made a great deal of money for himself, by changing ski makers. He sticks by K2, a local company close to his home at Yakima. The twins' toothpaste grin accompanies almost every K2 advertisement: 'Where I go my skis go too.' He is traditionalist, perhaps, rather than conservative. 'Alpine ski is a traditional sport like cross-country and jumping. You don't change things for the good of the media or the general public. You look at the Grand Prix circuit. It's basically the same as it always has been. You go out on the same dates to the same tracks year after year. I think ski-racing could be a lot better organised than it is. We went to places this year, and how they got World Cup races is beyond me. They don't have the facilities, let alone the hills, to have World Cup. That's very unfortunate for the sport and it's not right. Serge Lang's dream was to have a World Cup race at Markstein in Alsace. At Tarnaby we had another race because

Made it! Victory in the Aspen GS wrapped up Phil Mahre's third overall World Cup title

it was Ingemar's home town. Kranjska Gora in Yugoslavia where they start in 1983–4 was way too steep for GS. They weren't good hills. I think people should look at hills and what kind of races you can hold on them before they are scheduled for World Cup. We had some good races this year, but not so many quality ones as we had in the past because of the sites.'

Grand Prix motor-racing is perhaps a dangerous comparison. The circuit may be reasonably regular, but very little else is. Mahre, though, recognises the dangers of a situation where the ski industry, partly due to recession, has insufficient funds to support the ski circuit it has created. 'The ski industry has dropped out rapidly from what it was five years ago. Ski teams can't depend on those companies to support them as much as they did. At a team meeting last spring they said they wanted to raise at least another twenty per cent. I said there's no way you can ask these people for more money. They can't even afford what they're doing right now. Ski-racing is a great opportunity for people to advertise so you've got to go out and sell that, not go back and back to the same people. You've got to find people to put money into something to get something in return. In America it's you scratch my back and I'll scratch yours.'

Television, in his view, doesn't always help. 'This year they brought in the red line. You couldn't take your skis off till you crossed that line. I agree it was getting

Full stretch: Phil Mahre gets set for a downhill

a little bit out of hand, the way people were in more of a rush to get their skis off than they were to do anything. But if the skiers can get their skis on the television screen so that people can identify with them then more power to it. TV doesn't have the right to tell you that you can't do that. Without the manufacturers and sponsors the whole sport goes crack. If it goes too far they can turn the cameras off. The red line was just a big joke.'

Ski-racing is not a sport for day-dreaming. Mahre at times found himself doing just that as the 1982–3 season approached. 'Too often if you're a winner everyone wants a piece of your time, and the ski team doesn't utilise the rest of the athletes on the team well enough. I think Steve and I got called to do fifty per cent or more of the fund-raising, and it's quite a work load. That's something we'd just as soon not have, and yet the ski team just will not say no. So things are getting just a little bit out of hand. More and more you're having to live up to everybody's role, so you wear these clothes and you do this and that. . . . I've always been my own individual and now more and more people are trying to tell me how to run my life.' Mahre was fearful that the negative aspects were overtaking the positive.

Whereas he had exploded into the 1981–2 season, sewing up the overall title by 24 January and the individual slalom and GS titles by 26 March, at the 1982–3 Christmas break he trailed the overall leader Peter Mueller by fifty, with a miserable thirty points. Chief coach Konrad Rickenbach and slalom henchman Tom Kelly knew Mahre too well to reflect disappointment. 'He can make up at the back end,' said Kelly. 'We don't have a single regular GS until 14 January.' Meantime Mahre was working on his downhill. 'Skiing is work, but it's also fun,' he said. 'I want to win downhill if I can, and I will try to capitalise on slaloms combining with downhills as well as in traditional giant slalom.' He drily noted how the World Cup committee had excluded conventional GS from any pairing with downhill for combined points. At Val d'Isère Super G, his bête noir, was paired with downhill and at Madonna di Campiglio with special slalom. Wengen, Kitzbuehel and St Anton were the only events where he could score combined. Under the abstruse World Cup scoring system a skier counts his best three out of five combineds. Mahre, being Mahre, won all three he entered with a total of 75 points, which left everyone for dead in that division. In the 1983–4 season even that will be impossible since three of the five combineds include super.

An unkind questioner asked Doug Powell, the no. 1 US downhill specialist, what it was like to be relegated the moment Phil Mahre chose to ski downhill. Powell answered gallantly that it shed a lot of light on the downhill training programme to have the world's top skier giving advice on line. 'He's so experienced. He's never been in a wind tunnel but he just drops into the tuck. He's a wonderful natural athlete and I ski better when he's around.' Just what a Powell discusses with a Mahre provides a fascinating insight. 'We discuss different lines,' says Mahre. 'How to approach a particular turn and how to exit. Should you ride low and come out low, or high and come out high. So you want to turn low and you're going under a flag. You might carry more speed coming into the turn but you'll drop it going under the flag, or you drop some speed going high but you gain it going out. So you gain speed across the flag. There's a happy medium where you have to be on a course and how you approach certain gates and turns.'

But is it inches, feet or yards they're talking about? 'I'm talking sometimes about several yards. It depends on conditions. A foot here or there isn't going to make a difference. When you change a line it has to to be pretty drastic, meaning anything from six to ten feet. It's how long you delay before you start a turn, and the snow conditions make a big difference. Okay, a course is very hard and you have to go a little bit rounder and be a little bit higher. If the course is softer you can cut everything off and go a bit straighter. You have to visualise this and know

Italian breakthrough: Michael Mair scores Italy's first World Cup win in three years

about it, and you have to think that when you're on the course.'

A spluttering, stuttering season was a nightmare of scheduling and rescheduling. Poor snow, high wind and bad visibility so disrupted the downhill season that up to Kitzbuehel on 23 January only two races – the Hahnenkamm itself and Val Gardena on 19 December – had been held as planned. Mahre's resolution to ski downhill as hard and as well as possible was blighted only by the race's vulnerability to the weather. 'It represents such a frustration to train three days and then have the race cancelled because of weather,' he said. All the same, he skied the best downhill campaign of his career. The 28 points he scored from downhill may represent less than half the difference of 67 which finally separated him from the second-placed Stenmark, but without downhill he could not have scored the 75 combined points which crucially bolstered his total. At Madonna, Stenmark entered the one combined which put together Super G and special and, although placed seventy-fifth in the super, his worst-ever World Cup result, he was second in the slalom and managed eight points from eighth place.

Mueller won the first Super G at Val d'Isère, disproving one of Mahre's pre-season theories that downhillers stood little or no chance, and Italy's Michael

Above: Crashing down: Ingemar Stenmark in crash helmet for the Madonna Super G. He insisted on using his GS skis. *Below*: Crashing out: Stenmark takes a tumble at St Anton. He still went on to win his eighth overall special slalom title

New leader (*above*): Switzerland's Pirmin Zurbriggen, who won the Adelboden GS to take a short-lived overall lead. *Opposite*: Sharing the limelight: Stig Strand, Stenmark's boyhood rival, won two slaloms and equalled Stenmark's points total

Mair, another downhiller, won the second at Madonna, Italy's first World Cup victory for three years. It all added up to the fact that the Super favoured the downhiller. Subsequently it emerged that Stenmark had insisted on skiing the race on his giant slalom skis, which are a good 20 centimetres shorter than downhill skis, so his extreme tardiness was explained. Pirmin Zurbriggen briefly took the overall leadership from Mueller as the downhill peak gave way to the slaloms, and Stig Strand, a fellow-countryman of Stenmark, who skis only special slalom, won at Madonna and Furano to provide more piquancy. But slowly the wheels of the Mahre wagon got rolling. Steve won the slaloms at Parpan and St Anton although he had severely strained his left shoulder in a fall at an exhibition night slalom in Switzerland and was in agony every time he brushed a slalom pole.

A pole, according to the Oxford Dictionary, is a long, slender, rounded, tapering piece of wood or (rarely) metal. It is also a point in the celestial sphere about which the stars appear to revolve. For the Mahres, it is all of this and a good deal more. Phil's disastrous accident at Lake Placid in 1981 came when he hooked a ski around a pole. But the excitement of skiing, to them, is 'racing poles'. Not just any old poles. After Lake Placid the wood pole gave way to the hinged plastic, the

Yugoslav joy: Bojan Krizaj, winner of the second Markstein slalom. The pressure will be on at Sarajevo

hinge at the foot of the pole just above the snowline. It was an intended safety measure to reduce the incidence of injury such as Mahre had suffered. Quickly racers evolved a technique for it, seemingly shouldering through a pole while keeping the skis just inside its line. Mahre's comment is technically pertinent. 'I ski the same as I did before. I still believe you have to go round the pole, but it's more evident every day that on flatter hills you have to go through the pole. But I feel that if I go out and train with a breakaway pole I ski terrible. I start making major tactical mistakes and I have to go back and train with bamboo. I have to train with bamboo at least once a week otherwise I just forget how to ski. In a way the hinged pole has become a joke. It's ruined the sport. It should be left to organisers and racers whether they want bamboo or not.'

European speculation was still that the Mahres' results were suffering because of their family responsibilities. In the Park Hotel at Wengen you would see either one twin or the other nursing a babe more gently than a ski pole as he watched videos of runs or just brought up some wind. The powerful shoulders which can zap modern hinged gate poles like twigs were just another pillow. The padded

Sarajevo in his sights: Boris Strel, 1982 World Championship GS bronze medallist, another of the Yugoslav Olympic hopes

knees ripped by thousands of blows from bamboo practice poles provided just another warm seat. At Lauterbrunnen station, before first light, you would see the same pair humping heavy, awkward luggage across the railway lines to parked team trucks and cars while their wives sat patiently nursing the children on chilly station seats. Next would come the bouncing seven-hour journey to Kitzbuehel across the spine of the Alps. Continental pressmen speculated that while the wives and children made the twins happy it also confused them. Their relationship – super friend and super foe – might be disturbed by the presence of such important people in their lives. Was it an awkward decision for Marolt to break the unwritten 'no family' rules of touring groups? 'Not at all,' said Marolt. 'The Mahres are mature men. It was the natural thing to do.'

As the European tour began to tread unfamiliar territory, a resurgent Stenmark won the first special slalom at the Alsatian resort of Markstein and the giant slalom at the Black Forest village of Todtnau in three days. Mahre's record of five third places in slalom slipped to fifth at Markstein 2, but his fourth in the Todtnau GS was the best of his three conventional GS results so far. More than 10,000

Terror of Tarnaby: Andreas Wenzel won on Stenmark's home slope to 10,000 Swedes' distress

Swedes lined the slalom course of Stenmark's home town of Tarnaby, near the Arctic circle, on 23 February but were bitterly disappointed when their hero fell at the ninth gate set upon his nursery slope. Andreas Wenzel won the race from another Tarnaby native, Stig Strand, for his first victory in three years. Mahre missed a gate and with it went his chance of retaining the slalom title. Wenzel, with typical coolness, refused to accept that he had spoiled the party. 'If I lost to Ingemar in Liechtenstein it would be my fault, not Ingemar's.' Stenmark, on the other hand, could feel that 'Ingemarsbacken', the slope named after him, by dealing such a blow to Mahre, had in the end done him a good turn.

In Aspen, Colorado, it was Mahre's turn to face the pressures and advantages of home conditions. The World Cup's byzantine scoring system bemused many of his unversed press interrogators. Mahre had not won a race this season. What sort of hero was this? 'If the most consistent skier wins, it doesn't matter if he doesn't win races,' Phil told puzzled Superbowl experts. 'That's the scoring and it's who comes out on top that matters.' The more experienced you were, the better you skied, he explained. 'Racers used to stay around for four years, now it's eight.' Then something most of his questioners, pressing him on life after ski, could cotton on to: 'If you've been successful in sport you're inevitably going to be successful in anything else.' Just to reassure everyone, Phil picked up ninth

Not so lonely now: Ingemar Stenmark with his most constant companion, Ann Heggeveit

place in the Aspen downhill. Then, on 7 March, came the turning point.

Stenmark had been closing up fast with three wins in six races. Phil was only 28 points ahead, and after the first GS run on Ajax Mountain, Stenmark was a mere .13 of a second behind, poised for another famous charge. But anything Stenmark can do Phil believes he can do as well or better. 'There's a lot of skiers who ski on strength; you can't train or teach a person to be a winner,' says Mahre. 'That has to come from within. You need all the physical and athletic abilities together with the technique. But you've got to have the mental attitude or you'll never be a champion. In the start the guy that's ahead of me is the guy I watch. If he skis great then I feel great. If he skis terrible then I don't watch him, because it's very bad for me. If Stenmark has a good run then I know I can do that. I know that I can ski with Ingemar any day, so when he goes down and has a superb run I know that I'm capable of doing that.'

Now, on the second run, Stenmark skied in front of Mahre. It was a good run, 1:16.36, but not good enough. Mahre was next on, bearing a prophetic bib, no. 3, and set for a run to demolish Ingemar in a time of 1:15.89, and beating Girardelli, who had edged out the Swede. It gave him a total of 2:31.49 to win the overall World Cup for the third successive year. A day later Mahre won the Vail GS before the largest crowd ever to see World Cup in the USA. Former president

Above: Austrian slalom prospect: Christian Orlainsky, 21, second at Kitzbuehel. *Below*: Swiss newcomer: Max Julen ended an outstanding GS season second to Phil Mahre with five seconds, a third and a fourth

New record: Stenmark won his eighth overall special slalom title although Strand equalled his points total at Furano

Gerald Ford gave him his medal, but Furano, Japan, offered greater satisfaction still as his third successive win pushed him past Stenmark and the Swiss, Max Julen, for the giant slalom title. It was the title everyone said he could not win. Stenmark took the overall slalom title for a record eighth time, his points equal to Strand's but with more wins.

A satisfied Phil Mahre went home to Yakima. Next year, he said, he might do a Jack Nicklaus. Maybe play the tournaments he fancied, certainly go for his first Olympic gold at Sarajevo. He still hasn't anything specific in mind after skiing. 'But I know I have the mental make-up to succeed. There's not a worry about failure.' And anything he couldn't do? 'Oh well . . . sitting in an office. I need to be outside and very busy. I like to be my own boss.' Is he comfortably off for life? 'Right now, I can't say that, but I've made some investments and I hope they'll pay off. I think I've been very lucky to be as successful in my sport as I have, and that there was that sort of money. When I first started there wasn't any money. I was there at the right time, because actually I think there's less money today. But by no means will I take advantage of it. I've fought hard for everything I've got in life and this is no exception.' Steve announced during the summer that 1983–4 would be his last year, but Phil might carry on, especially if he won the World Cup again. 'No one has ever won five,' he said. Phil Mahre is the man who can.

6

CRYSTAL FROM THE BLUE GRASS

Nicholas Howe

When Christopher Columbus left his home in Genoa to seek the New World, there was no ski area in nearby Limone Piemonte. There is now, and on the first sunny day of the 1983 World Cup season flags and pennants snapped in the breeze, grand opera played on the slalom hill, a thousand children left school to cheer their team, and a line of brightly coloured laundry was hung out to dry between the bottom lift-tower and the corner of the timing hut by the finish. Italian racers stood second and third after the first run, but by day's end it was Hanni Wenzel and Erika Hess holding up the hands of the winner, Tamara McKinney. Three months later those two held up Tamara's hands again. The perennial Hanni had won the combined and placed second overall, Erika had the slalom title and placed third overall, and Tamara was taking the GS title and the World Cup home to the New World.

Tamara McKinney's rise to the top of international skiing was not a surprise. 'We were in America in 1977 and I saw this very tiny girl,' said a German coach. 'I thought "My God, look at those turns!" If she ever gets big enough, we are really in trouble.' That was her first World Cup race, and she was fourteen. Four years later she won the World Cup GS title.

This precocious assault came from a double athletic heritage. Tamara's father Rigan was a famous steeplechase jockey in Kentucky, and her mother Frances was (and is) an enthusiastic skier. Tamara is the youngest of seven children and when she was still a baby Mrs McKinney moved them to a winter base in western Nevada and got a part-time job as a ski instructor at Mt Rose. A person of principle and strong character, Frances had her family and household declared a legally independent school and educated the children herself through the primary and secondary grades, all the while taking them skiing every afternoon. Four of them made it to the national team level of competition, and her son Steve went on to lead speed skiing into the modern era.

Tamara was taken up the mountain every day by Sven Coomer, the ski-school director and formerly a coach on the international circuit. But Coomer wasn't

'Watch water running down a hill. Tamara skis like that.' Tamara McKinney began the season with second place in the GS and Combined at Val d'Isère. Four months and seven victories later the World Cup was hers

American grin: Tamara McKinney, the first non-European to win the women's World Cup since Nancy Greene in 1968, celebrates another win

interested in racing then: 'I just wanted Tamara to get in as many miles as possible, to enjoy the thrill of skiing and skiing well and smoothly and lightly and have a really good time on skis.' Those days were the basis of her most admired asset today: her 'touch', her ability to sense the snow under her feet.

Coomer was succeeded as Mt Rose ski-school director by Anderl Molterer, the 'Blitz from Kitz' who led the Austrian juggernaut through the 1950s. When Tamara was about ten, Molterer began her serious education for racing: 'Such a tough little skier,' he recalls, 'you could hardly see her in the bumps. And what a worker – up the hill again and again!' With Molterer, Tamara began to learn her other leading asset: a canny sense of course strategy.

Both those qualities were abundantly present on the day of the St Gervais GS last winter. 'I was so happy there,' she says, 'so ready to go do something that I had to remind myself not to use it all up on the training hill. I was having such a good time and the snow was so good that I had to sort of gather that happiness up and save it for the race.' Tamara did manage to save some: she was first at both interval times, both finishes, and the totals. Like Erika Hess, she isn't particularly

Swiss grit: Doris de Agostini – a triumph of determination over probability at 6′ 1″

self-conscious about technique, and her instinct for line is so natural and unaffected that when she's at her best she hardly seems to be racing at all. 'Watch water running down a hill,' says a coach. 'Tamara skis like that.'

1983 was the first time the women's World Cup overall title had left Europe since Nancy Greene in 1967 and 1968, and the season saw other wonders as well. It was the year of the first new event since 1950, the year that France returned as a major power, the year that the four oldest women on the circuit rivalled the teenagers for positions on the trophy steps all winter long. And it saw the worst weather in memory – Alpine monsoons and one memorable blizzard forced schedule changes for fourteen of the twenty-six events.

The first comet portending these unsettled times was sighted over the battlements of Val d'Isère at the opening downhill. Doris de Agostini won, but Elisabeth Chaud, Marie-Luce Waldmeier and Caroline Attia of France scored points. The historic Austro–Swiss downhill empire tottered again in the next race at Sansicario, Italy, when Attia, Claudine Emonet, Catherine Quittet and Françoise Bozon led the field, with Germany's Heidi Wiesler in third. This was a bitterly

Downhill all the way: Doris de Agostini wins Les Diablerets, her third victory of the season

protested event: the first fifteen skied in a dead flat light, a critical factor on the subtle terrain of that course. After eighteen finishers it looked like the first win for Canada's Laurie Graham, with de Agostini in fourth. Then the leaders looked to their laurels as the sun came out, a cool breeze glazed the course, and the second and third seeds held what was essentially a different race. 'Like a dream,' said Attia, and many would agree: Graham was pushed back to eleventh and de Agostini salvaged just one point for fifteenth. It happened again in the Pfronten race transferred to Schruns: de Agostini won, but Chaud and Attia were right behind, with Waldmeier in ninth.

If Sansicario was a dream for Attia, the Schruns downhill defies easy description of any sort. In fact, most journalists got it wrong. Training started on ice, then the Pfronten make-up was run in a gathering snowstorm. The next day was worthy of Lear's madness and everything – fences, gates and course – simply disappeared. The third day was still so bad that the men's slalom at Wengen was cancelled by avalanche danger, and at Schruns some people got lost riding up the T-bar. But the plucky women soldiered on, though the drifts were so deep that some sections of their slalom were set in steep narrow hallways shovelled through the snow.

The organisers at Schruns were determined to run their downhill, and announced it for the next day. What followed was widely reported as a racers' boycott, but it

Gallic glory: Caroline Attia won Sansicario and the French finished second, fourth and fifth as well

wasn't. The coaches joined the jury in an early-morning inspection. The jury saw that continuous work by the tractor crews had maintained a firm surface and announced an 11 a.m. start; the coaches saw that the gates had been taken up to let the tractors work and some had been put back two or three metres away from their original sites, and that drifting snow had substantially altered the course contour. It was, they argued, a different course from the one their teams had trained on and raced three days earlier, and they sent the racers down to the hotels. The jury said the course was in good condition, and moved the start up to 1 p.m. The coaches signed a protocol stating their position (Austria abstaining) and the jury sent the forerunners up to the start. Then, for probably the first time in World Cup history, first-seed racers sat in their hotels and watched forerunners on the course with the clock showing times on the screen.

It was a difficult situation. Weather conditions were improving on the mountain, but there was no time for a new cycle of training – the downhillers were due in Megève the next day. Serge Lang, chairman of the World Cup committee, was in touch and he sided with the jury, stating that since it was a coaches' initiative that interrupted the race the FIS was not obliged to stage a substitute race. The racers were angry because they stood to lose both the race and the combined; the Schruns organisers were angry because they were losing a race they'd worked hard for; and

French breakthrough: Elisabeth Chaud (*above*), Claudine Emonet (*below*) and Catherine Quittet (*opposite*), together with Attia and Marie-Luce Waldmeier, all finished in the top fifteen of the downhill overall

the coaches were unhappy for both groups but felt they had to protect their teams from an unsafe situation. The next day Lang announced there would be a substitute race after all, at Megève. Having been provided with a fuller account of the situation, he now sided with the coaches and overturned the FIS technical director's decision. So there were two downhills at Megève: Maria Walliser led America's Maria Maricich the first day, Elisabeth Kirchler led de Agostini the second, but there were French women in third both days, with five other scoring team-mates.

It was the vindication of an unusual tactic. The overwhelmingly successful French team of the 1960s had followed the example of other skiing powers and succumbed to a palace revolution as the decade turned. It takes a long time to rebuild a development programme, and for many years the winter fortunes of the French were in the dependable but lonely hands of Fabienne Serrat and Perrine Pelen. Then the women embarked on a daring gambit: they decided to steal a march on the rest of the women's field and build their downhill training around films of the Austrian and Canadian *men* on their race courses. This produced some unforgettable training scenes as they worked on the radical inside move the men use in turns, but by the end of the 1983 downhill season seven French women had scored twenty-four times, and that without the help of the 1982 title-holder, Marie-Cécile Gros-Gaudenier, who was twentieth in the first race, then went out for the season after a training crash the next week.

Olympic prospects: Maria Walliser (*above*), winner at Megève 1 and Sarajevo, and Elisabeth Kirchler (*below*), winner of Megève 2 and second at Sarajevo, have the qualities needed for Olympic gold

New World success: Laurie Graham (*above*) won her first downhill on home-ground Mont Tremblant, while Cindy Nelson (*below*) took the second Verbier Super G, her first win since 1979

Reconstructed knee: Maria Maricich, a brave second at Megève 1 after a two-year struggle to come back

The North American downhill momentum did not carry into 1983. The Canadians lost Diana Haight and Dianne Lehodey early in the season and Graham's win on home-ground Mont Tremblant was their only top-three trophy. The best US finish was the second placing put in by Maricich at Megève, a fine achievement that capped her two-year fight to come back from a total knee reconstruction, with 19-year-olds Pam Ann Fletcher and Debbie Armstrong leading the veterans behind her. Switzerland's Walliser, also 19, continued her drive of 1982 and finished second in the standings, while Kirchler of Austria – yet another member of the exceptional class of 1963 – placed third on the year. (The Austrians look to her as their veteran leader – their *average* age in 1983 was $17\frac{1}{2}$!)

The courses themselves deserve mention. None of the 1983 downhills was as long as the shortest of the year before, none had as much vertical as the lowest profile seen in 1982, and 1983 winners spent on average 20.06 seconds less time on the course than in 1982. These developments worked very much against the interests of such classically trained downhillers as Cindy Nelson, Irene Epple and

Evergreen veteran: Hanni Wenzel won the last slalom of the season at Furano to finish second overall

Gerry Sorensen, and helped open up the scoring ranks: 38 per cent more bib numbers above 30 were on the scoring lists than the year before.

Doris de Agostini prevailed in these changing times – a triumph of determination over probability. Doris is 6 ft 1 in tall, and in one year of her rise through the ranks she grew $11\frac{1}{2}$ inches, a biomechanical assault that does not lend itself to athletic greatness. Co-ordination problems aside, a long slender frame cannot develop much leverage or muscular force. This made the willowy Doris a natural glider but, as she said, 'my turns were terrible – I could not hold at all – and in 1979 I almost gave up'. Her problem was partly due to a largely unrecognised fact of life: the taller skiers are, the narrower their natural stance tends to be (*vide*

Smile please: Irene Epple (*left*) and Doris de Agostini

Christa Kinshofer and the late Alexander Zhirov, tragically killed in a car crash in April 1983). This condition was so extreme with de Agostini that she actually made some high-speed turns on her inside ski, the other one up in the air like an outrigger. She won a race in 1976, then kept working until she finished second in 1981 and 1982, and finally won in 1983. Then she retired.

The gate racers' first job in the new season was to learn how to recognise a GS course when they saw one. The sometimes mercurial FIS had decreed a longer, more open course formula in the spring of 1982, so the teams concentrated on that during their summer and autumn training. Then, just two days before the first race at Val d'Isère, the FIS restored the old formula. Then, after sponsoring the unofficial début of the Super Giant Slalom at the 1982 finals, they changed the formula for that race also.

The men had a distinctly grumpy response to the new event, but among the women everyone from de Agostini to Zini charged into the two Super Gs held on successive days at Verbier – everyone, that is, except Erika Hess, who was recovering from an arthroscopic tune-up of her knee over Christmas. Let history show that Zoe Haas of Switzerland was the first woman down an official Super G course, and that she gilded the lily of her classic heritage with

Combined harvester: Hanni Wenzel skis the Val d'Isère downhill for valuable Combined points

a token of more recent New World minting: a sticker on her skis said, in English, 'No Problem!'

Few finish orders have ever been so revealing. In recent years summer bulldozers, winter grooming tractors, and changing fashions among course setters have conspired to produce shorter, straighter and smoother downhills. The older generation of racers complained that they were becoming technologically unemployed – that the skills needed to master the big booming turns, the bumps, dips and compressions of their youth no longer counted for much. Some cynics put this down to the rearguard defence of a fading career, but they were silenced by the finish order of the first Super G: Irene Epple won, followed by Hanni Wenzel, Tamara McKinney, Cindy Nelson and Fabienne Serrat – the classic skills of the four oldest women on the circuit bracketing the best pure natural talent of the era. 'I like it,' said Epple, 'I really do. It's very demanding: you have to set up as if for a GS turn, but then you have to stand on that outside ski for what seems like a very long time. And the speeds are much higher than one is used to, so it takes courage as well as technique, and I think that is the essence of racing.' The next day Canada's Currie Chapman set a somewhat faster course on the same hill and even the most partisan European journalists hailed the victory of '*die alte*

Holding the fort: Perrine Pelen (*above*) and Fabienne Serrat (*opposite*), mainstays of the French team for a decade

Amerikanerin', as Cindy Nelson had her first win since 1979, followed by Haas, Epple, McKinney and Wenzel.

The seven regular GS races were oddly spaced, five coming in the last two weeks of the season. Erika Hess had overtaken McKinney's first-run lead to win the opener in Val d'Isère, then on 23 January at St Gervais, McKinney and Christin Cooper simply ran away from the field: the two Americans were first and second at both intervals, both finishes, and the totals. But the women didn't see another GS until 6 March, when France's Anne-Flore Rey won at Mont Tremblant in Canada.

The intervening period saw dizzying fortunes on the slalom circuit. After the Verbier Super GS the gate racers went to Davos. This pearl among the jewels of the alpine tiara had never staged a World Cup race before and they only got this one on two and a half days' notice, but no one will ever forget it. There were brass bands, roast chestnuts by the finish line, and the steepest race course anyone had ever seen, with mattresses padding the trees and downhill crash nets to keep the women from the awful abyss. McKinney led Hess, Pelen and Cooper at the finish – 'the first time,' said Perrine Pelen, 'that I have ever raced on a waterfall.'

French polish: Fabienne Serrat, skiing as well as ever in her eleventh year on the circuit

The brilliant sun and high spirits of Davos gave way to the storm-lashed corridors at Schruns, where McKinney, Cooper, Hess, Konzett, Zini, Wenzel and Pelen were all knocked out of the race, to name but a few of the 48 disqualifieds and did not finishes, and Pelen's wrenching crash left her at reduced efficiency for the rest of the year. But the finish order confirmed the emergence of what is in effect a sub-set of the first slalom seed – what a turf accountant would call 'mudders'. Anni Kronbichler and Roswitha Steiner of Austria and the Tlalka twins from Poland filled four of the five top spots. Slalom traditionally favours small quick women like Hess and McKinney, whereas the two Austrian women and the Tlalkas are very much larger and more powerfully framed, with a rather rough stand-up style that doesn't approach the technical sophistication of their smaller peers. But it seemed well suited to the uncertain footing in the chunky ice, soft ruts and gravel patches that distinguished the 1983 season, and those four shared two wins and twenty-five other scores, the quality of the points varying inversely with the conditions underfoot.

The blizzard of Schruns turned out to be just a warm-up for the next slalom, at Diablerets, run in such heavy rain that Hanni Wenzel declared it the worst race

Super ski: Irene Epple (*above*) won the first-ever women's Super G at Verbier. Erika Hess (*below*), despite a season disrupted by injury, could still take the slalom title with two victories and three of four second places

Solidarity on skis: the Polish twins Malgorzata (*left*) and Dorota Tlalka, whose powerful stand-up style brought results in the slalom

day she'd seen in twelve years. There were six inches of clear water on one side of the finish area before the race, a condition which did nothing for a troupe of sixteen pre-race go-go dancers the sponsors had positioned there to hoof it up to the beat of such old Swiss favourites as the Benny Goodman version of 'Sing Sing Sing' from the famed Carnegie Hall concert of 1938, then 'Good Morning, Good Morning' – a happy-face tune of more recent origin. And, to add a more authentic feeling to the proceedings, the Austrian punk-rock team of Steiner, Kronbichler, and Ladstaetter turned up with glitter, decals and grease paint on their faces and their hair spiked with red yarn. The happiness, if not the dancing, became general after the race as the brass band gurgled with the rain flooding their horns while Italy's Paoletta Magoni broke into a baton-twirling act and the leaders poured water from their trophies.

Those few people in dry enough places to apply pencil to paper found that the race had been won by Maria Rosa Quario. Hanni Wenzel clinched the 1983 Combined title here, closely followed by Elisabeth Kirchler of Austria. Kirchler is a natural downhiller, perhaps the best three-event skier in the rising generation, and an all-round favourite. This day she splashed across the finish soaking wet, hair streaming in her face, and flung wide her arms in a typically

Slalom winners all: Maria Rosa Quario (*above*) won at Les Diablerets and Vysoke Tatry, while Anni Kronbichler (*below*) and Roswitha Steiner (*opposite*) were first-time winners for Austria at Schruns and Waterville Valley

grand and generous salute: 'I am here!' she shouted, partly out of her normal exuberance, and perhaps also in surprise that her sturdy downhiller's approach to the nuances of slalom had got her so far.

One day at Sarajevo, Lisi, Lea Soelkner and their woman trainer were waiting in the parking lot up at the mountain. The weather was awful, as usual, and the transportation wasn't working, also as usual, so I offered them a lift down to the hotel. We got all their skis lashed onto the big top racks of the US Subaru and Lea and the trainer got into the back, with Lisi in front. A Brandenburg concerto was in the stereo tape deck, so I switched it on, turned up the heater, and started to pick my way down the road – which was unploughed, also as usual.

Soothed by the heat and the music, the two in the back promptly went to sleep. But there were scattered knots of Yugoslavs at the side of the road peering at us through the swirling gloom and that was all Kirchler needed. She reached over and turned up the elegant music, then went into her Queen Elizabeth act. She gave those patented little waves first to the left, then to the right, with that patented little parade-route smile fastened on her face. The bewildered Yugoslavs stared in through the windows, but she was not at all discouraged by this lack of public acclaim. Without disturbing the little smile, she muttered, 'You

Unlucky year: Christin Cooper, overall third in 1982, broke a leg in downhill training at Les Diablerets

know, Nick – I am very popular everywhere I go. Just look how they love me here!' I suggested that the tumultuous throngs lining the ceremonial avenues could see her better if she were up on the roof, and she said, 'Oh, you think so? That's probably right!' Whereupon she popped the latch on the door and started to jump out, but I was able to save her royal dignity before she made it up onto the roof.

Diablerets was a sad camp for the Americans. Christin Cooper broke her leg in a freak accident while training downhill, and the next day Maria Maricich broke her collar bone in the race. Tamara McKinney had a disappointing sixth in the slalom, which left her one point ahead of Wenzel in the overall, and 25 points ahead of Erika Hess. Then she failed to finish the next three races while Erika placed first, second and third for a scoring advantage of 60 to nothing. Back home in America on 8 March, Tamara faced a slalom and three GSs in five days. It was, as American sportscasters like to say, 'the season'.

Some national team coaches put brutal pressure on their leading skiers, but not the Americans. Two staff members found a moment to talk to Tamara: 'Look,' they said, 'if the season ended right now we'd be happy, so just don't worry about the rest. If it happens, it happens, and if it doesn't we're still happy and proud –

Still-life study: Brigitte Oertli, Erika Hess and Maria Rosa Quario inspect the course at Limone

it's still been a great year.' 'That was nice,' said Tamara later, 'it reminded me to keep things in perspective.' Thus refreshed, she took second in the slalom and won all three GS races.

As the teams left for Japan, Tamara had clinched the GS title, but the overall still hung on a complex balance: Erika could overtake her if she won both the slalom and GS in Furano and Tamara failed to score at all. The odds against this were lengthened by the history of the GS hill there: it has a notorious 25-second flat that actually goes uphill at the end, greatly favouring the larger and heavier racers who carry speed better – Nadig won the last two races here and Wenzel won this one.

Tamara fell at the last gate above the flats and at the 30-second interval she was 3.5 seconds behind. Incredibly, she finished just 0.11 behind Erika's tenth place, and that gave her the World Cup. The next day she celebrated by taking the slalom for her seventh win of the season, and the crystal globe went to Lexington, Kentucky – long the capital of thoroughbred racing in America, and now the home of the women's skiing World Cup.

Erika Hess won two slalom races and was, characteristically, second in the four others that she finished. One key to Erika's success has always been her *evenness*,

Gold in 1984? Erika Hess

her ability to stay balanced on almost any surface or course. And, as so often happens, her racing style is a metaphor of her personality: unfailingly friendly and gracious, she gives no hint of whether she's had a first place or a DNF. Partisan journalists expected her to win almost every race in 1983 and when she didn't they had a ready supply of excuses for her. But she turned away every one they offered: 'The course was very good. . . . No, I didn't have any mistakes. . . . I think I ski spring poles very well. . . .' Finally, after the last race in Japan, she answered them one last time and achieved the kind of laurel a stopwatch can never certify: 'No,' said Erika, 'I didn't lose the World Cup. Tamara won it.'

LEADING WORLD SKIERS

In the following biographical information on world skiers seeded in the top fifteen of each discipline at the start of the 1983–4 season or with two or more top-ten finishes in the 1982–3 season the skier's name is followed by his nationality, date of birth and home town. World Cup overall positions are then listed, followed by top-ten results in World Championships and Olympic Games. Finally 1982–3 World Cup results in the top ten are given (preceded by the date 1983).

The following abbreviations are used: WC – World Championships; OG – Olympic Games; Dh – Downhill; Sl – Slalom; GS – Giant Slalom; Comb – Combined. In the overall results the last two figures of the year only are used. Nationalities for biographies and records are indicated by the normal FIS system:

AUS Australia
AUT Austria
BRD West Germany
BUL Bulgaria
CAN Canada
DAN Denmark
FRA France
GBR Great Britain
HUN Hungary
ITA Italy
JPN Japan
JUG Yugoslavia
LIE Liechtenstein
LUX Luxembourg
MEX Mexico
NOR Norway
POL Poland
SOV USSR
SPA Spain
SUI Switzerland
SWE Sweden
TCH Czechoslovakia
USA United States

MEN

Vladimir Andreev

Grega Benedik

Andreev, Vladimir, SOV
9.2.58, Noskh-Murmansk.
Overall: 1979 – 91; 80 – 51; 81 – 20; 82 – 84; 83 – 85. WC 82: Sl 10th.

Benedik, Grega, JUG
10.5.62, Zirovnica.
Overall: 1983 – 51; **1983** GS: 9th Madonna di Campiglio; 10th Gällivare; 10th Furano.

Brooker, Todd, CAN
24.11.59, Paris, Ont.
Overall: 1982 – 32; 83 – 27. **1983** Dh: 6th Val Gardena 1; 1st Kitzbuehel 2; 1st Aspen.

Buergler, Thomas, SUI
3.3.60, Rickenbach.
Overall: 1983 – 40. **1983** GS: 5th Val d'Isère; 9th Adelboden; 8th Kranjska Gora; 7th Vail.

Buergler, Toni, SUI
17.8.57, Rickenbach.
Overall: 1979 – 20; 80 – 49; 81 – 24; 82 – 22; 83 – 56. WC 82: Dh 8th. **1983** Dh: 9th Pontresina; 10th St Anton.

Todd Brooker

Thomas Buergler

Toni Buergler

Conradin Cathomen

Ivano Edalini

Roberto Erlacher

Canac, Michel, FRA
2.8.56, Bourg d'Oisans.
Overall: 1981 – 98; 82 – 87; 83 – 31. WC 82: Comb 5th. **1983** Sl: 9th Madonna di Campiglio; 7th Parpan; 9th Kitzbuehel; 3rd Kranjska Gora; 4th St Anton; 7th Furano. Comb: 9th Madonna di Campiglio.

Cathomen, Conradin, SUI
2.6.59, Laax.
Overall: 1981 – 50; 82 – 28; 83 – 14 (Dh 2nd). WC 82: Dh 2nd. **1983** Dh: 4th Pontresina; 9th Val Gardena 1; 1st Val Gardena 2; 3rd Val d'Isère 1; 1st Val d'Isère 2; 8th Aspen; 3rd Lake Louise.

de Chiesa, Paolo, ITA
14.3.56, Saluzzo.
Overall: 1975 – 10; 76 – 40; 77 – 49; 78 – 23; 80 – 45; 81 – 36; 82 – 16; 83 – 27. WC 82: Sl 4th. **1983** Sl: 7th Courmayeur; 5th Madonna di Campiglio; 4th Parpan; 5th Kitzbuehel; 4th Kranjska Gora; 2nd Markstein 1; 8th Tarnaby; 6th Gällivare; 4th Furano.

Edalini, Ivano, ITA
20.8.61, Colle Valtrompia.
Overall: 1982 – 52; 83 – 38. **1983** Sl: 10th Madonna di Campiglio; 5th St Anton; 5th Tarnaby.

Enn, Hans, AUT
10.5.58, Hinterglemm.
Overall: 1976 – 55; 77 – 35; 78 – 38; 79 – 12; 80 – 7 (GS 2nd); 81 – 14; 82 – 13; 83 – 20. WC 78: GS 6th. OG 80: Sl 4th; GS 3rd. WC 82: GS 6th. **1983** GS: 6th Val d'Isère; 2nd Madonna di Campiglio; 1st Kranjska Gora; 3rd Garmisch-Partenkirchen; 9th Aspen; 5th Vail; 4th Furano.

Erlacher, Roberto, ITA
16.9.63, Colfoso.
Overall: 1983 – 29. **1983** GS: 4th Kranjska Gora; 10th Garmisch-Partenkirchen; 8th Todtnau; 7th Aspen; 4th Vail; 7th Furano. Comb: 7th Madonna di Campiglio.

Fjaellberg, Bengt, SWE
15.9.61, Tarnaby.
Overall: 1981 – 32; 82 – 59; 83 – 34. WC 82: Sl 3rd. **1983** Sl: 8th St Anton; 8th Markstein 1; 2nd Markstein 2; 7th Gällivare.

Michel Canac

Paolo de Chiesa

Hans Enn

Bengt Fjaellberg

Jure Franko

Joel Gaspoz

Marc Girardelli

Klaus Heidegger

Franko, Jure, JUG
28.3.62, Nova Gorica.
Overall: 1980 – 68; 82 – 59; 83 – 32. **1983** GS: 7th Val d'Isère; 6th Madonna di Campiglio; 5th Adelboden; 9th Kranjska Gora; 8th Garmisch-Partenkirchen; 7th Gällivare; 5th Aspen.

Frommelt, Paul, LIE
9.8.57, Schaan.
Overall: 1976 – 55; 77 – 10 (Sl 3rd); 78 – 33; 79 – 17; 80 – 26; 81 – 17; 82 – 31; 83 – 41. WC 78: Sl 3rd. **1983** Sl: 5th Kranjska Gora; 6th St Anton; 9th Markstein 1; 10th Tarnaby.

Gaspoz, Joel, SUI
25.9.62, Morgins.
Overall: 1980 – 17; 81 – 11; 82 – 7; 83 – 77. OG 80: GS 7th. WC 82: Sl 5th; GS 4th.

Giorgi, Alex, ITA
9.12.58, Selva.
Overall: 1982 – 47; 83 – 35. **1983** Sl: 9th Tarnaby; 8th Furano. GS: 6th Kranjska Gora; 6th Aspen; 10th Vail.

Girardelli, Marc, LUX
18.7.63, Trintange.
Overall: 1980 – 84; 81 – 26; 82 – 6 (GS 3rd); 83 – 4. **1983** Sl: 10th Courmeyeur; 4th Kitzbuehel; 7th St Anton; 5th Markstein 1; 4th Tarnaby; 1st Gällivare. GS: 7th Adelboden; 10th Kranjska Gora; 9th Garmisch-Partenkirchen; 6th Todtnau; 2nd Aspen. Comb: 2nd Kitzbuehel; 3rd Kitzbuehel/Markstein; 4th St Anton.

Gruber, Franz, AUT
8.11.59, Molln.
Overall: 1979 – 32; 80 – 45; 81 – 25; 82 – 15; 83 – 9. WC 82: Sl 8th. **1983** Sl: 7th Madonna di Campiglio; 5th Parpan; 1st Kranjska Gora; 10th St Anton; 7th Markstein 1; 6th Tarnaby; 9th Gällivare; 5th Furano. GS: 8th Gällivare; 6th Vail. Comb: 3rd Madonna di Campiglio.

Heidegger, Klaus, AUT
19.8.57, Goetzens.
Overall: 1976 – 49; 77 – 2; 78 – 4 (Sl 2nd); 80 – 32; 83 – 46. **1983** Sl: 7th Kranjska Gora.

Heinzer, Franz, SUI
11.4.62, Rickenbach.
Overall: 1981 – 36; 82 – 26; 83 – 26. WC 82: Dh 4th. **1983** Dh: 4th

Paul Frommelt

Alex Giorgi

Franz Gruber

Franz Heinzer

Helmut Hoeflehner

Max Julen

Thomas Kerschbaumer

Bojan Krizaj

Val Gardena 1; 7th Val Gardena 2. GS: 4th Val d'Isère; 4th Madonna di Campiglio. Comb: 1st Val d'Isère/Val Gardena.

Hoeflehner, Helmut, AUT
24.11.59, Gumpenberg.
Overall: 1980 – 53; 81 – 30; 82 – 24; 83 – 24. **1983** Dh: 5th Pontresina; 9th Val Gardena 2; 10th Kitzbuehel 1; 9th Sarajevo; 3rd Aspen; 1st Lake Louise. Comb: 7th Val d'Isère/Val Gardena.

Johnson, Bill, USA
30.3.60, Van Nuys, Ca.
Overall: 1983 – 65. **1983** Dh: 6th St Anton.

Julen, Max, SUI
25.3.61, Zermatt.
Overall: 1982 – 45; 83 – 8 (GS 2nd). **1983** Sl: 9th Courmayeur; 10th Parpan. GS: 2nd Adelboden; 2nd Kranjska Gora; 2nd Todtnau; 2nd Gällivare; 4th Aspen; 3rd Vail; 2nd Furano.

Kernen, Bruno, SUI
25.3.61, Schoenried.
Overall: 1983 – 22. **1983** Dh: 10th Val Gardena 1; 7th Val d'Isère 2; 1st Kitzbuehel 1; 7th Kitzbuehel 2; 10th Lake Louise. Comb: 4th Kitzbuehel; 6th Kitzbuehel/Markstein.

Kerschbaumer, Thomas, ITA
23.6.64, Cortina.
Overall: 1983 – 52. **1983** GS: 10th Madonna di Campiglio; 6th Garmisch-Partenkirchen.

Klammer, Franz, AUT
3.12.53, Mooswald.
Overall: 1973 – 8; 74 – 5 (Dh 2nd); 75 – 3 (Dh 1st); 76 – 4 (Dh 1st); 77 – 3 (Dh 1st); 78 – 5 (Dh 1st); 79 – 51; 80 – 33; 81 – 40; 82 – 14; 83 – 18 (Dh 1st). WC 74: Dh 2nd; GS 10th; Comb 1st. OG 76: Dh 1st. WC 78: Dh 7th. WC 82: Dh 7th. **1983** Dh: 2nd Pontresina; 1st Val Gardena 1; 3rd Val Gardena 2; 5th Val d'Isère 2; 6th Kitzbuehel 2; 3rd Sarajevo; 8th St Anton; 2nd Lake Louise.

Krizaj, Bojan, JUG
3.1.57, Kranj.
Overall: 1977 – 43; 78 – 20; 79 – 8 (GS 3rd); 80 – 4 (Sl 2nd); 81 – 6 (Sl 3rd); 82 – 9; 83 – 9. OG 80: 4th. WC 82: Sl 2nd; GS 7th. **1983** Sl: 5th

Bill Johnson

Bruno Kernen

Franz Klammer

Courmayeur; 4th Madonna di Campiglio; 10th Markstein 1; 1st Markstein 2; 3rd Tarnaby; 5th Gällivare; 3rd Furano. GS: 9th Val d'Isère; 4th Adelboden. Comb: 4th Madonna di Campiglio.

Lee, Steven, AUS
7.8.62, Sydney.
Overall: 1983 – 48. **1983** Dh: 10th Kitzbuehel 1. Comb: 8th Kitzbuehel/Markstein; 8th St Anton.

Peter Luescher

Jacques Luethy

Phil Mahre

Steven Lee

Luescher, Peter, SUI
14.10.56, Romanshorn.
Overall: 1975 – 52; 76 – 25; 77 – 36; 78 – 16; 79 – 1 (GS 2nd); 80 – 10; 81 – 58; 82 – 28; 83 – 5. OG 76: Sl 8th. WC 82: Comb 2nd. **1983** Dh: 2nd Val d'Isère 1; 7th Kitzbuehel 1; 8th Kitzbuehel 2; 6th Sarajevo; 1st St Anton. GS: 2nd Val d'Isère; 1st Garmisch-Partenkirchen. Comb: 3rd Val d'Isère/Val Gardena; 3rd Kitzbuehel; 5th Kitzbuehel/Markstein; 5th St Anton.

Luethy, Jacques, SUI
11.7.59, Charmey.
Overall: 1979 – 13; 80 – 6 (GS 3rd); 81 – 15; 82 – 19; 83 – 17. OG 80: Sl 3rd; GS 5th. **1983** Sl: 2nd Parpan; 6th Markstein 1; 8th Markstein 2. GS: 3rd Adelboden; 7th Kranjska Gora; 7th Garmisch-Partenkirchen; 6th Gällivare. Comb: 6th Madonna di Campiglio.

Mader, Guenther, AUT
24.6.64, Brenner.
Overall: 1983 – 56. **1983** GS: 7th Madonna di Campiglio; 10th Aspen.

Mahre, Phil, USA
10.5.57, Yakima, Wash.
Overall: 1976 – 14; 77 – 9; 78 – 2 (Sl 3rd; GS 3rd); 79 – 3 (Sl 2nd); 80 – 3; 81 – 1 (Sl 2nd; GS 3rd); 82 – 1 (Sl 1st; GS 1st); 83 – 1 (GS 1st). OG 76: GS 5th. OG 80: Sl 2nd; GS 10th. **1983** Dh: 5th St Anton; 9th Aspen. Sl: 3rd Courmayeur; 3rd Madonna di Campiglio; 3rd St Anton; 3rd Markstein 1; 5th Markstein 2; 4th Gällivare; 6th Furano. GS: 5th Kranjska Gora; 4th Todtnau; 2nd Gällivare; 1st Aspen; 1st Vail; 1st Furano. Comb: 1st Kitzbuehel; 1st Kitzbuehel/Markstein; 1st St Anton.

Mahre, Steve, USA
10.5.57, Yakima, Wash.
Overall: 1976 – 27; 77 – 43; 78 – 23; 79 – 10; 80 – 12; 81 – 4 (Sl 3rd); 82 – 3 (Sl 3rd); 83 – 12. WC 78: Sl 8th. WC 82: GS 1st. **1983** Sl: 4th Courmayeur; 8th Madonna di Campiglio; 1st Parpan; 6th Kitzbuehel; 1st St Anton. GS: 8th Vail. Comb: 3rd St Anton.

Mair, Michael, ITA
13.2.62, Brunico.
Overall: 1982 – 42; 83 – 21. WC 82: Dh 10th. **1983** Dh: 5th Val

Vladimir Makeev

Guenther Mader

Steve Mahre

Michael Mair

Silvano Meli

Peter Mueller

Christian Orlainsky

Steve Podborski

d'Isère 1; 4th Sarajevo; 2nd Aspen. GS: 1st Madonna di Campiglio.

Makeev, Vladimir, SOV
10.9.57, Kemehovo.
Overall: 1979 – 41; 81 – 48; 82 – 66; 83 – 46. WC 78: Dh 9th. WC 82: Dh 6th. **1983** Dh: 8th Pontresina; 10th Val d'Isère 2.

Meli, Silvano, SUI
11.8.60, Leysin.
Overall: 1982 – 21; 83 – 19. **1983** Dh: 7th Val d'Isère 1; 9th Val d'Isère 2; 8th Kitzbuehel 1; 4th Kitzbuehel 2; 10th Sarajevo; 2nd St Anton. Comb: 5th Kitzbuehel; 7th Kitzbuehel/Markstein; 7th St Anton.

Mueller, Peter, SUI
6.10.57, Adliswil.
Overall: 1977 – 24; 78 – 36; 79 – 15 (Dh 1st); 80 – 9 (Dh 1st); 81 – 5 (Dh 3rd); 82 – 4 (Dh 2nd); 83 – 7. WC 78: Dh 5th. OG 80: Dh 4th. WC 82: Dh 5th. **1983** Dh: 3rd Pontresina; 2nd Val Gardena 1; 4th Val d'Isère 2; 4th Kitzbuehel 1; 4th Kitzbuehel 2; 6th Aspen; 4th Lake Louise. GS: 1st Val d'Isère. Comb: 2nd Val d'Isère/Val Gardena; 9th Kitzbuehel.

Orlainsky, Christian, AUT
17.2.62, Tschagguns.
Overall: 1979 – 26; 80 – 18; 81 – 10; 82 – 27; 83 – 15. **1983** Sl: 6th Courmayeur; 6th Madonna di Campiglio; 2nd Kitzbuehel; 3rd Markstein 2; 9th Furano. GS: 10th Val d'Isère. Comb: 2nd Madonna di Campiglio.

Pfaffenbichler, Gerhard, AUT
26.3.61, Unken.
Overall: 1981 – 28; 82 – 46; 83 – 37. **1983** Dh: 1st Sarajevo; 10th Aspen; 7th Lake Louise.

Podborski, Steve, CAN
25.7.57, Don Mills, Ont.
Overall: 1976 – 43; 78 – 31; 79 – 36; 80 – 30; 81 – 9 (Dh 2nd); 82 – 8 (Dh 1st); 83 – 30. OG 80: Dh 3rd. WC 82: Dh 9th. **1983** Dh: 2nd Kitzbuehel 1; 9th Kitzbuehel 2; 2nd Sarajevo; 4th St Anton.

Popangelov, Peter, BUL
31.1.59, Samokov.
Overall: 1977 – 58; 78 – 13; 79 – 19; 80 – 13; 81 – 50; 82 – 59; 83 – 42. OG 80: Sl 6th. **1983** Sl: 10th Kitzbuehel; 9th St Anton; 10th Markstein 2; 7th Tarnaby.

Raeber, Urs, SUI
28.11.58, Wilderswil.
Overall: 1982 – 78; 83 – 15. **1983** Dh: 10th Pontresina; 3rd Val Gardena 1; 4th Val Gardena 2; 9th Val d'Isère 1; 6th Val d'Isère 2; 3rd Kitzbuehel 1; 2nd Kitzbuehel 2; 7th Sarajevo; 7th Aspen; 9th Lake Louise. Comb: 5th Val d'Isère/Val Gardena; 7th Kitzbuehel; 9th Kitzbuehel/Markstein.

Urs Raeber

Gerhard Pfaffenbichler

Peter Popangelov

Erwin Resch

Resch, Erwin, AUT
4.3.61, Mariapfarr.
Overall: 1979 – 63; 81 – 42; 82 – 12; 83 – 25. WC 82: Dh 3rd. **1983** Dh: 2nd Val Gardena 2; 1st Val d'Isère 1; 5th Aspen; 4th Lake Louise.

Hubert Strolz

Sbardellotto, Danilo, ITA
23.10.60, S. Lucia (Sondrio).
Overall: 1983 – 48. **1983** Dh: 3rd Val d'Isère 2. Comb: 10th Val d'Isère/Val Gardena.

Ingemar Stenmark

Stenmark, Ingemar, SWE
18.3.56, Monte Carlo.
Overall: 1974 – 12; 75 – 2 (Sl 1st; GS 1st); 76 – 1 (Sl 1st; GS 1st); 77 – 1 (Sl 1st; GS 2nd); 78 – 1 (Sl 1st; GS 1st); 79 – 5 (Sl 1st; GS 1st); 80 – 2 (Sl 1st; GS 1st); 81 – 2 (Sl 1st; GS 1st); 82 – 2 (Sl 2nd; GS 2nd); 83 – 2 (Sl 1st; GS 2nd). WC 74: GS 9th. OG 76: GS 3rd. WC 78: Sl 1st; GS 1st. OG 80: Sl 1st; GS 1st. WC 82: Sl 1st; GS 2nd. **1983** Sl: 1st Courmayeur; 2nd Madonna di Campiglio; 1st Kitzbuehel; 1st Markstein 1; 6th Markstein 2; 3rd Gällivare. GS: 7th Adelboden; 3rd Kranjska Gora; 1st Todtnau; 1st Gällivare; 3rd Aspen; 2nd Vail; 3rd Furano.

Danilo Sbardellotto

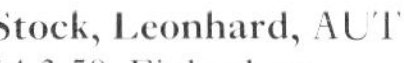

Leonhard Stock

Stock, Leonhard, AUT
14.3.58, Finkenberg.
Overall: 1977 – 31; 78 – 21; 79 – 2; 80 – 45; 81 – 12; 82 – 18; 83 – 33. OG 80: Dh 1st. **1983** Dh: 8th Val Gardena 1; 8th Val Gardena 2; 10th Val d'Isère 1; 7th St Anton; 6th Lake Louise. GS: 9th Furano.

Stoelzl, Fritz, AUT
22.2.61, Weisskirchen.
Overall: 1983 – 54. **1983** Dh: 8th Val d'Isère 1; 8th Val d'Isère 2.

Fritz Stoelzl

Stig Strand

Strand, Stig, SWE
25.8.56, Tarnaby.
Overall: 1976 – 55; 77 – 46; 79 – 68; 80 – 59; 81 – 31; 82 – 34; 83 – 11 (Sl 1st). **1983** Sl: 2nd Courmayeur; 1st Madonna di Campiglio; 7th Kitzbuehel; 2nd Kranjska Gora; 4th Markstein 2; 2nd Tarnaby; 2nd Gällivare; 1st Furano.

Strel, Boris, JUG
20.10.59, Skofja Loka.
Overall: 1979 – 25; 80 – 25; 81 – 21; 82 – 34; 83 – 36. OG 80: GS 8th. WC 82: GS 3rd. **1983** GS: 6th Todtnau; 5th Gällivare; 9th Vail; 6th Furano.

Boris Strel

Strolz, Hubert, AUT
26.6.62, Zams.
Overall: 1982 – 20; 83 – 39. WC 82: GS 10th. **1983** GS: 5th Madonna di Campiglio; 5th Garmisch-Partenkirchen. Comb: 5th Madonna di Campiglio.

Toetsch, Oswald, ITA
17.1.64, Val-di-Vizze.
Overall: 1983 – 94.

Vion, Michel, FRA
22.10.59, Pralognan.
Overall: 1982 – 35; 83 – 65. WC 82: Comb 1st.

Weirather, Harti, AUT
25.1.58, Reutte.
Overall: 1979 – 53; 80 – 15; 81 – 8 (Dh 1st); 82 – 10 (Dh 2nd); 83 – 13 (Dh 3rd). OG 80: Dh 9th. WC 82: Dh 1st. **1983** Dh: 1st Pontresina; 5th Val Gardena 1; 6th Val Gardena 2; 6th Val d'Isère 1; 5th Kitzbuehel 1; 3rd St Anton; 4th Aspen. GS: 8th Val d'Isère; 8th Madonna di Campiglio. Comb: 4th Val d'Isère/Val Gardena.

Wenzel, Andreas, LIE
18.3.58, Planken.
Overall: 1977 – 21; 78 – 3 (GS 2nd); 79 – 6; 80 – 1; 81 – 7; 82 – 5; 83 – 3 (Sl 3rd). OG 76: Sl 10th; Comb. 5th. WC 78: GS 2nd; Comb. 1st. OG 80: GS 2nd. **1983** Dh: 9th St Anton. Sl: 3rd Parpan; 2nd St Anton; 4th Markstein 1; 7th Markstein 2; 1st Tarnaby; 2nd Furano. GS: 6th Adelboden; 4th Garmisch-Partenkirchen; 5th Todtnau. Comb: 2nd Kitzbuehel/Markstein; 2nd St Anton.

Wirnsberger, Peter, AUT
13.9.58, Vordernberg.
Overall: 1977 – 24; 78 – 17; 79 – 16; 80 – 19; 81 – 18; 82 – 23; 83 – 43. OG 80: Dh 2nd. **1983** Dh: 7th Pontresina; 10th Val Gardena 2; 10th Kitzbuehel 2; 8th Lake Louise.

Zurbriggen, Pirmin, SUI
4.2.63, Saas Almagell.
Overall: 1981 – 32; 82 – 11; 83 – 6. **1983** Dh: 9th Kitzbuehel 1. Sl: 8th Courmayeur. GS: 3rd Val d'Isère; 3rd Madonna di Campiglio; 1st Adelboden; 2nd Garmisch-Partenkirchen; 3rd Todtnau; 9th Gällivare; 8th Aspen; 5th Furano. Comb: 1st Madonna di Campiglio; 6th Val d'Isère/Val Gardena; 4th Kitzbuehel/Markstein.

Oswald Toetsch

Michel Vion

Harti Weirather

Andreas Wenzel

Peter Wirnsberger

Pirmin Zurbriggen

WOMEN

Debbie Armstrong

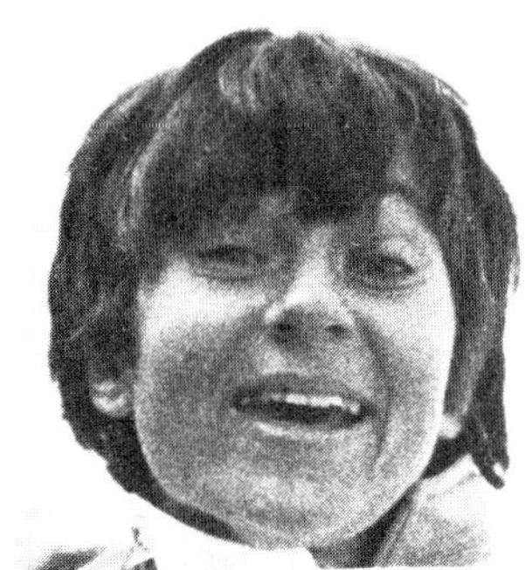
Caroline Attia

Armstrong, Debbie, USA
6.12.63, Seattle, Wa.
Overall: 1983 – 33. **1983** Dh: 7th Sansicario; 5th Les Diablerets.

Attia, Caroline, FRA
4.7.60, Fontenay.
Overall: 1983 – 21. **1983** Dh: 1st Sansicario; 3rd Schruns; 3rd Megève 2; 9th Les Diablerets.

Barbier, Hélène, FRA
3.7.66, St Etienne.
Overall: 1983 – 44. **1983** Sl: 8th Waterville Valley. GS: 5th Val d'Isère; 7th Verbier 1.

Hélène Barbier

Olga Charvatova

Charvatova, Olga, TCH
11.6.62, Gottwaldov.
Overall: 1979 – 17; 80 – 34; 81 – 15; 82 – 26; 83 – 8. WC 78: Comb 9th. WC 82: Sl 9th; Comb 5th. **1983** Dh: 4th Sarajevo; 8th Mt Tremblant. Sl: 6th Schruns; 10th Vysoke Tatry; 6th Waterville Valley. GS: 6th Mt Tremblant; 9th Vail; 7th Furano. Comb: 10th Val d'Isère; 1st Schruns.

Chaud, Elisabeth, FRA
7.12.60, Puy St Vincent.
Overall: 1979 – 69; 81 – 41; 82 – 11; 83 – 17. **1983** Dh: 5th Val d'Isère; 2nd Schruns; 5th Sarajevo. GS: 8th Verbier 1; 7th Verbier 2.

Christin Cooper

Cooper, Christin, USA
8.10.59, Sun Valley, Id.
Overall: 1977 – 35; 78 – 18; 79 – 23; 80 – 18; 81 – 4 (Sl 2nd); 82 – 3 (Sl 3rd); 83 – 12. OG 80: Sl 8th; GS 7th. WC 82: Sl 2nd; GS 2nd; Comb 3rd. **1983** Sl: 3rd Piancavallo; 4th Davos. GS: 9th Val d'Isère; 2nd Megève. Comb: 1st Sansicario.

Elisabeth Chaud

Sylvia Eder

Eder, Sylvia, AUT
24.8.65, Leogang.
Overall: 1981 – 51; 82 – 21; 83 – 24. **1983** Dh: 8th Val d'Isère; 8th Megève 1; 8th Les Diablerets. Comb: 2nd Schruns; 7th Les Diablerets.

Ehrat, Ariane, SUI
17.2.61, Schaffhausen.
Overall: 1982 – 55; 83 – 37. **1983** Dh: 8th Sansicario; 7th Megève 2; 3rd Sarajevo.

Ariane Ehrat

Claudine Emonet

Emonet, Claudine, FRA
13.2.62, Praz-sur-Arly.
Overall: 1982 – 53; 83 – 30. **1983** Dh: 2nd Sansicario; 5th Megève 2; 8th Sarajevo.

Michaela Gerg

Epple, Irene, BRD
18.6.57, Seeg-Allgau.
Overall: 1973 – 41; 74 – 34; 75 – 13; 76 – 10; 77 – 18; 78 – 11; 79 – 3 (GS 3rd); 80 – 5; 81 – 5 (GS 3rd); 82 – 2 (GS 1st); 83 – 6. OG 76: Dh 10th. WC 78: Dh 2nd; GS 4th. OG 80: GS 2nd. WC 82: Dh 8th; Comb 7th. **1983** Dh: 10th Val d'Isère; 6th Schruns. GS: 1st Verbier 1; 3rd Verbier 2; 5th Megève; 8th Waterville Valley 1; 10th Waterville Valley 2; 10th Vail. Comb: 6th Val d'Isère; 8th Sansicario/Piancavallo; 5th Schruns; 5th Les Diablerets.

Irene Epple

Epple, Maria, BRD
11.3.59, Seeg-Allgau.
Overall: 1976 – 38; 77 – 33; 78 – 7; 80 – 29; 81 – 14; 82 – 4 (GS 2nd); 83 – 9 (GS 3rd). WC 78: GS 1st. OG 80: GS 8th. WC 82: Sl 6th. **1983** Sl: 6th Limone Piemonte; 5th Piancavallo; 9th Davos; 10th Schruns; 9th Les Diablerets; 7th Maribor. GS: 8th Val d'Isère; 6th Verbier 1; 6th Verbier 2; 9th Megève; 2nd Mt Tremblant; 2nd Waterville Valley 1; 2nd Waterville Valley 2; 5th Vail; 8th Furano.

Maria Epple

Figini, Michela, SUI
7.4.66, Prato-Leventina.
Overall: 1983 – 26. **1983** Dh: 3rd Mt Tremblant. GS: 4th Waterville Valley 2; 7th Vail. Comb: 10th Schruns; 10th Les Diablerets.

Michela Figini

Fjeldstad, Torill, NOR
22.2.58, Lillehammer.
Overall: 1980 – 36; 81 – 20; 82 – 41. OG 80: Dh 7th. WC 82: Dh 4th.

Torill Fjeldstad

Flanders, Holly Beth, USA
26.12.57, Deerfield, NH.
Overall: 1979 – 29; 80 – 23; 81 – 20; 82 – 12 (Dh 2nd); 83 – 54. WC 82: Dh 9th. **1983** Dh: 8th Megève 1.

Holly Beth Flanders

Gantnerova-Soltysova, Jana, TCH
30.9.59, Kezmarok.
Overall: 1976 – 40; 79 – 33; 80 – 13; 81 – 21; 82 – 63; 83 – 29. OG 80: 10th Dh. **1983** Dh: 6th Sansicario; 7th Schruns; 5th Megève 1; 6th Megève 2; 9th Sarajevo. Comb: 8th Val d' Isère.

Jana Gantnerova-Soltysova

Laurie Graham

Marie-Cécile Gros-Gaudenier

Zoe Haas

Erika Hess

Gerg, Michaela, BRD
10.11.65, Lenggries.
Overall: 1982 – 66; 83 – 15. **1983** Dh: 4th Megève 1; 7th Megève 2. GS: 9th Waterville Valley 1; 9th Waterville Valley 2. Comb: 2nd Les Diablerets.

Graham, Laurie, CAN
30.3.60, Inglewood, Ont.
Overall: 1980 – 23; 81 – 52; 82 – 29; 83 – 18. WC 82: Dh 3rd. **1983** Dh: 6th Val d'Isère; 4th Schruns; 10th Les Diablerets; 6th Sarajevo; 1st Mt Tremblant. Comb: 7th Val d'Isère.

Gros-Gaudenier, Marie-Cecile, FRA
18.6.60, Mont-Saxonnex.
Overall: 1979 – 43; 80 – 64; 81 – 37; 82 – 15 (Dh 1st).

Gutensohn, Katrin, AUT
12.3.66, Kirchberg.
Overall: 1983 – 47. **1983** Comb: 7th Sansicario/Piancavallo; 7th Schruns.

Haas, Zoe, SUI
24.1.62, Engelberg.
Overall: 1979 – 49; 80 – 69; 81 – 24; 82 – 34; 83 – 25. **1983** GS: 2nd Verbier 2; 8th Megève. Comb: 8th Schruns; 8th Les Diablerets.

Haight, Diana, CAN
28.4.64, Fruitvale, BC.
Overall: 1982 – 46; 83 – 75.

Hess, Erika, SUI
6.3.62, Grafenort.
Overall: 1978 – 28; 79 – 15; 80 – 7; 81 – 2 (Sl 1st; GS 3rd); 82 – 1 (Sl 1st; GS 3rd); 83 – 3 (Sl 1st). WC 78: GS 9th. OG 80: Sl 3rd. WC 82: Sl 1st; GS 1st; Comb 1st. **1983** Sl: 2nd Limone Piemonte; 1st Piancavallo; 2nd Davos; 1st Maribor; 2nd Vysoke Tatry; 2nd Furano. GS: 1st Val d'Isère; 6th Megève; 3rd Mt Tremblant; 4th Waterville Valley 1; 5th Waterville Valley 2; 3rd Vail; 10th Furano. Comb: 3rd Val d'Isère; 2nd Sansicario/Piancavallo.

Hess, Monika, SUI
24.5.64, Grafenort.
Overall: 1982 – 38; 83 – 35. **1983** Sl: 9th Maribor; 4th Waterville Valley. GS: 6th Waterville Valley 1; 8th Waterville Valley 2.

Christa Kinshofer

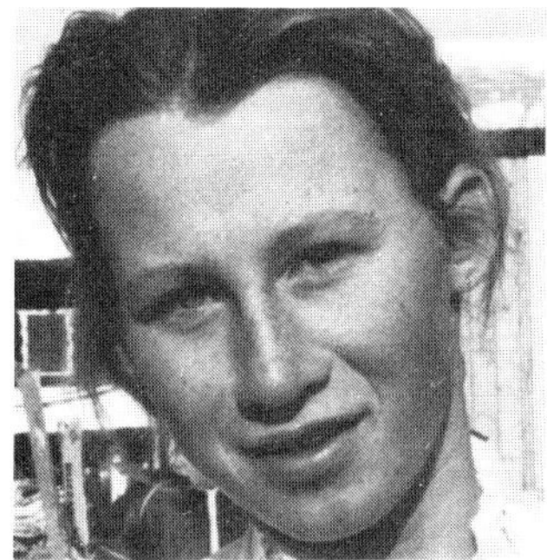

Katrin Gutensohn

Diana Haight

Monika Hess

Elisabeth Kirchler

Ursula Konzett

Anni Kronbichler

Tamara McKinney

Kinshofer, Christa, BRD
24.1.61, Miesbach.
Overall: 1977 – 40; 79 – 8 (GS 1st); 80 – 11; 81 – 9; 82 – 24; 83 – 66. OG 80: Sl 2nd; GS 5th. WC 82: GS 9th.

Kirchler, Elisabeth, AUT
17.11.63, Lanersbach.
Overall: 1981 – 33; 82 – 27; 83 – 4 (Dh 3rd). WC 82: Dh 6th; GS 8th. **1983** Dh: 6th Val d'Isère; 1st Megève 1; 2nd Les Diablerets; 2nd Sarajevo. GS: 4th Val d'Isère; 9th Mt Tremblant; 6th Vail; 4th Furano. Comb: 1st Val d'Isère; 9th Sansicario/Piancavallo; 3rd Les Diablerets.

Konzett, Ursula, LIE
15.11.59, Triesen.
Overall: 1977 – 28; 78 – 22; 79 – 40; 80 – 25; 81 – 38; 82 – 6 (Sl 2nd); 83 – 30. OG 76: Comb 5th. WC 82: GS 3rd. **1983** Sl: 7th Limone Piemonte; 5th Vysoke Tatry; 5th Furano. GS: 7th Val d'Isère.

Kronbichler, Anni, AUT
22.3.63, Walchsee.
Overall: 1980 – 64; 81 – 56; 82 – 22; 83 – 11. WC 82: Comb 6th. **1983** Sl: 9th Limone Piemonte; 10th Piancavallo; 1st Schruns; 7th Les Diablerets; 3rd Maribor; 6th Waterville Valley; 10th Furano. GS: 9th Verbier 2; 4th Mt Tremblant. Comb: 4th Sansicario/Piancavallo.

Lehodey, Dianne, CAN
11.3.60, Calgary, Alb.
Overall: 1982 – 41.WC 82: Dh 5th.

McKinney, Tamara, USA
16.10.62, Olympic Valley, Ca.
Overall: 1979 – 25; 80 – 14; 81 – 6 (GS 1st); 82 – 9; 83 – 1 (Sl 2nd; GS 1st). WC 82: GS 6th. **1983** Sl: 1st Limone Piemonte; 1st Davos; 6th Les Diablerets; 2nd Waterville Valley; 1st Furano. GS: 2nd Val d'Isère; 3rd Verbier 1; 4th Verbier 2; 1st Megève; 1st Waterville Valley 1; 1st Waterville Valley 2; 1st Vail. Comb: 2nd Val d'Isère; 6th Les Diablerets.

Magoni, Paoletta, ITA
14.9.64, Selvino.
Overall: 1982 – 76; 83 – 39. **1983** Sl: 8th Limone Piemonte; 6th Piancavallo; 8th Davos; 8th Furano.

Maricich, Maria, USA
30.3.61, Sun Valley, Id.
Overall: 1983 – 48. **1983** Dh: 2nd Megève 1.

Merle, Carole, FRA
24.1.64, Super-Sauze.
Overall: 1982 – 71; 83 – 38. **1983** Dh: 10th Megève 1. GS: 3rd Megève; 5th Furano.

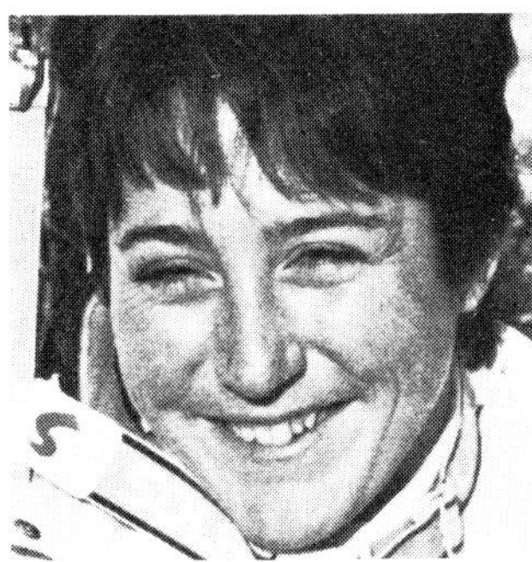

Carole Merle

Dianne Lehodey

Paoletta Magoni

Maria Maricich

Cindy Nelson

Brigitte Oertli

Heidi Preuss

Moesenlechner, Regine, BRD
1.4.61, Siegsdorf.
Overall: 1975 – 39; 78 – 28; 79 – 12; 80 – 15; 81 – 21; 82 – 69; 83 – 79. WC 78: Sl 10th.

Nelson, Cindy, USA
19.8.55, Lutsen, Minn.
Overall: 1974 – 15; 75 – 8; 76 – 8; 77 – 19; 78 – 5 (Dh 2nd); 79 – 4; 80 – 10; 81 – 8; 82 – 5; 83 – 7 (GS 2nd). OG 76: Dh 3rd; Comb 4th. WC 78: Dh 5th; Comb 6th. OG 80: Dh 7th. WC 82: Dh 2nd; Comb 4th. **1983** Dh: 7th Sarajevo. GS: 4th Verbier 1; 1st Verbier 2; 10th Megève; 5th Waterville Valley 1; 3rd Waterville Valley 2; 2nd Vail; 6th Furano. Comb: 9th Val d'Isère; 6th Schruns; 4th Les Diablerets.

Oak, Cindy, USA
21.4.61, Orchard Park, NY.
Overall: 1980 – 73; 81 – 39; 82 – 59. WC 82: Dh 10th.

Oertli, Brigitte, SUI
10.6.62, Egg.
Overall: 1982 – 59; 83 – 35. **1983** Dh: 9th Sansicario. Comb: 6th Sansicario/Piancavallo; 4th Schruns.

Pelen, Perrine, FRA
3.7.60, Corenc Mt Fleury.
Overall: 1977 – 7 (Sl 2nd); 78 – 6 (Sl 2nd); 79 – 9; 80 – 4 (Sl 1st; GS 2nd); 81 – 6 (Sl 3rd); 82 – 8; 83 – 16. WC 78: Sl 4th; GS 8th. OG 80: GS 3rd. WC 82: Comb 2nd. **1983** Sl. 2nd Piancavallo; 3rd Davos; 10th Les Diablerets. GS: 10th Verbier 1; 8th Vail; 9th Furano.

Preuss, Heidi, USA
18.3.61, Lakeport, NH.
Overall: 1979 – 18; 80 – 12; 81 – 30; 82 – 50; 83 – 65. OG 80: Dh 4th.

Quario, Maria Rosa, ITA
24.5.61, Milan
Overall: 1979 – 13; 80 – 31; 81 – 18; 82 – 10; 83 – 14 (Sl 3rd). OG 80: Sl 4th. WC 82: Sl 5th. **1983** Sl: 4th Limone Piemonte; 9th Piancavallo; 2nd Schruns; 1st Les Diablerets; 1st Vysoke Tatry.

Quittet, Catherine, FRA
22.1.64, Flumet.
Overall: 1983 – 43. **1983** Dh: 4th Sansicario; 4th Mt Tremblant.

Regine Moesenlechner

Cindy Oak

Perrine Pelen

Maria Rosa Quario

Catherine Quittet

Fabienne Serrat

Gerry Sorensen

Dorota Tlalka

Rey, Anne-Flore, FRA
2.2.62, Brignoud.
Overall: 1982 – 44; 83 – 20. **1983** GS: 10th Val d'Isère; 9th Verbier 1; 7th Megève; 1st Mt Tremblant; 5th Waterville Valley 2; 4th Vail.

Serrat, Fabienne, FRA
5.7.56, Alpe d'Huez.
Overall: 1973 – 20; 74 – 5 (GS 2nd); 75 – 5 (GS 3rd); 76 – 7; 77 – 9; 78 – 4 (Sl 3rd); 79 – 6; 80 – 6; 81 – 10; 82 – 18; 83 – 13. WC 74: Dh 10th; Sl 4th; GS 1st; Comb 1st. WC 78: Sl 5th; GS 6th; Comb 3rd. OG 80: GS 4th. WC 82: Sl 10th; GS 5th. **1983** Sl: 8th Schruns. GS: 6th Val d'Isère; 5th Verbier 1; 8th Verbier 2; 4th Megève; 3rd Waterville Valley 1; 2nd Furano. Comb: 3rd Schruns.

Soelkner, Lea, AUT
24.12.58, Tauplitz.
Overall: 1976 – 32; 77 – 15; 78 – 9; 79 – 11 (Sl 3rd); 80 – 17; 81 – 31; 82 – 6; 83 – 32. WC 78: Sl 1st. **1983** Dh: 2nd Val d'Isère; 7th Megève 2.

Sorensen, Gerry, CAN
15.10.58, Kimberley, BC.
Overall: 1981 – 45; 82 – 12; 83 – 39. WC 82: Dh 1st. **1983** Dh: 4th Val d'Isère; 5th Schruns; 7th Megève 1.

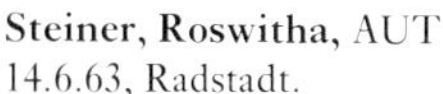

Steiner, Roswitha, AUT
14.6.63, Radstadt.
Overall: 1980 – 69; 81 – 49; 82 – 23; 83 – 23. WC 82: Sl 7th; GS 10th. **1983** Sl: 6th Davos; 5th Schruns; 4th Les Diablerets; 4th Vysoke Tatry; 1st Waterville Valley; 6th Furano.

Tlalka, Dorota, POL
27.4.63, Zakopane.
Overall: 1980 – 78; 81 – 76; 82 – 36; 83 – 28. WC 82: Sl 4th. **1983** Sl: 8th Piancavallo; 4th Schruns; 3rd Les Diablerets; 6th Maribor; 8th Vysoke Tatry; 10th Waterville Valley; 7th Furano.

Tlalka, Malgorzata, POL
27.4.63, Zakopane.
Overall: 1982 – 30; 83 – 22. WC 82: Comb 9th. **1983** Sl: 2nd Schruns; 3rd Vysoke Tatry; 5th Waterville Valley; 3rd Furano.

Anne-Flore Rey

Lea Soelkner

Roswitha Steiner

Malgorzata Tlalka

Veronika Vitzthum

Maria Walliser

Petra Wenzel

Heidi Wiesler

Vitzthum, Veronika, AUT
11.3.63, Unken.
Overall: 1982 – 66; 83 – 39. **1983** Dh: 10th Schruns; 3rd Les Diablerets; 8th Mt Tremblant.

Waldmeier, Marie-Luce, FRA
1.7.60, Annemasse.
Overall: 1982 – 39; 83 – 39. **1983** Dh: 8th Val d'Isère; 9th Schruns; 3rd Megève 1.

Walliser, Maria, SUI
27.5.63, Mosnang.
Overall: 1981 – 12; 82 – 17; 83 – 5 (Dh 2nd). **1983** Dh: 3rd Val d'Isère; 8th Schruns; 1st Megève 1; 10th Megève 2; 4th Les Diablerets; 1st Sarajevo; 2nd Mt Tremblant. GS: 10th Verbier 2; 7th Mt Tremblant; 7th Waterville Valley 2; 3rd Furano. Comb: 5th Val d'Isère.

Wenzel, Hanni, LIE
14.12.56, Schaan.
Overall: 1972 – 40; 73 – 5; 74 – 3; 75 – 2; 76 – 9; 77 – 5; 78 – 1 (Sl 1st; GS 2nd); 79 – 2; 80 – 1 (Dh 3rd; Sl 2nd; GS 1st); 81 – 3 (GS 3rd); 82 – 19; 83 – 2. WC 74: Sl 1st; GS 7th; Comb 2nd. OG 76: Sl 3rd; Comb 3rd. WC 78: Sl 6th; GS 5th; Comb 2nd. OG 80: Dh 2nd; Sl 1st; GS 1st. **1983** Sl: 3rd Limone Piemonte; 4th Piancavallo; 5th Davos; 2nd Les Diablerets; 2nd Maribor; 3rd Waterville Valley; 4th Furano. GS: 3rd Val d'Isère; 2nd Verbier 1; 5th Verbier 2; 10th Waterville Valley 1; 1st Furano. Comb. 4th Val d'Isère; 3rd Sansicario/Piancavallo; 1st Les Diablerets.

Wenzel, Petra, LIE
20.11.61, Planken.
Overall: 1979 – 48; 80 – 48; 81 – 46; 82 – 25; 83 – 19. WC 82: GS 4th. **1983** Sl: 7th Davos; 5th Les Diablerets; 4th Maribor; 7th Vysoke Tatry. GS: 5th Mt Tremblant.

Wiesler, Heidi, BRD
28.3.60, Staufen.
Overall: 1982 – 53; 83 – 33. **1983** Dh: 3rd Sansicario. Comb: 5th Sansicario/Piancavallo; 9th Schruns.

Winkler, Sieglinde, AUT
30.3.66, Ferlach.
Overall: 1982 – 50; 83 – 45. **1983** Dh: 10th Sansicario; 4th Megève 2; 7th Les Diablerets.

Marie-Luce Waldmeier

Hanni Wenzel

Sieglinde Winkler

Anja Zavadlav

Zavadlav, Anja, JUG
11.5.60, Ljubljana.
Overall: 1979 – 68; 80 – 59; 81 – 49; 82 – 31; 83 – 49. **1983** Sl: 9th Vysoke Tatry.

Zini, Daniela, ITA
30.5.59, Livigno.
Overall: 1979 – 14; 80 – 9; 81 – 11 (Sl 3rd); 82 – 31; 83 – 26. OG 80: Sl 7th. WC 82: Sl 3rd; GS 7th; Comb 8th. **1983** Sl: 8th Les Diablerets; 5th Maribor; 6th Vysoke Tatry; 9th Waterville Valley; 9th Furano.

Daniela Zini

WORLD CUP RECORDS 1983

MEN'S OVERALL 1983

1	Phil Mahre	USA	285
2	Ingemar Stenmark	SWE	218
3	Andreas Wenzel	LIE	177
4	Marc Girardelli	LUX	168
5	Peter Luescher	SUI	164
6	Pirmin Zurbriggen	SUI	161
7	Peter Mueller	SUI	125
8	Max Julen	SUI	116
9	Franz Gruber	AUT	112
	Bojan Krizaj	JUG	112
11	Stig Strand	SWE	110
12	Steve Mahre	USA	108
13	Harti Weirather	AUT	102
14	Conradin Cathomen	SUI	100
15	Christian Orlainsky	AUT	99
	Urs Raeber	SUI	99
17	Jacques Luethy	SUI	96
18	Franz Klammer	AUT	95
19	Silvano Meli	SUI	85
20	Hans Enn	AUT	84
21	Michael Mair	ITA	78
22	Bruno Kernen	SUI	77
23	Ken Read	CAN	76
24	Helmut Hoeflehner	AUT	74
25	Erwin Resch	AUT	73
26	Franz Heinzer	SUI	72
27	Todd Brooker	CAN	67
	Paolo de Chiesa	ITA	67
29	Robert Erlacher	ITA	65
30	Steve Podborski	CAN	63
31	Michel Canac	FRA	59
32	Jure Franko	JUG	56
33	Leonhard Stock	AUT	55
34	Bengt Fjaellberg	SWE	49
35	Alex Giorgi	ITA	47
36	Boris Strel	JUG	43
37	Gerhard Pfaffenbichler	AUT	40
38	Ivano Edalini	ITA	39
39	Hubert Strolz	AUT	38
40	Thomas Buergler	SUI	36
41	Paul Frommelt	LIE	34
42	Peter Popangelov	BUL	33
43	Peter Wirnsberger	AUT	32
44	Lars-Goeran Halvarsson	SWE	27
45	Frank Woerndl	BRD	26
46	Klaus Heidegger	AUT	23
	Vladimir Makeev	SOV	23
48	Steven Lee	AUS	22
	Danilo Sbardellotto	ITA	22
	Joze Kuralt	JUG	22
51	Grega Benedik	JUG	21
52	Siegfried Kerschbaumer	ITA	19
53	Hans Pieren	SUI	18
54	Odd Soerli	NOR	16
	Fritz Stoelzl	AUT	16
56	Toni Buergler	SUI	15
	Guenther Mader	AUT	15
	Hannes Spiss	AUT	15
59	Joergen Sundqvist	SWE	13
	Stefan Niederseer	AUT	13
61	Johan Wallner	SWE	12
	Bernhard Flaschberger	AUT	12
63	Egon Hirt	BRD	11
	Peter Mally	ITA	11
65	Bill Johnson	USA	10
	Uli Spiess	AUT	10
	Bernhard Fahner	SUI	10
	Gerard Rambaud	FRA	10
	Michel Vion	FRA	10
	Patrick Lamotte	FRA	10
71	Didier Bouvet	FRA	9
	Daniel Fontaine	FRA	9
	Sepp Wildgruber	BRD	9
74	Petr Soltys	TCH	8
	Helmut Gstrein	AUT	8
	Paul-Arne Skajem	NOR	8
77	Marco Tonazzi	ITA	7
	Martin Bell	GBR	7
	Joel Gaspoz	SUI	7
80	Daniel Mougel	FRA	6
	Antal Gotzy	HUN	6
	Florian Beck	BRD	6
	Mads Boedker	DAN	6
	Hubertus von Hohenlohe	MEX	6
85	Vladimir Andreev	SOV	5
	Peter Duerr	BRD	5
	Andras Voelgyesi	HUN	5
	Guido Hinterseer	AUT	5
	Torsten Jakobsson	SWE	5
90	Robin McLeish	CAN	4
	Naomine Iwaya	JPN	4
92	Tomaz Cerkovnik	JUG	3
	Hiroaki Ohtaka	JPN	3
94	Toshihiro Kaiwa	JPN	2
	Martin Hangl	SUI	2
	Tris Cochrane	USA	2
	Oswald Totsch	ITA	2
	Mike Brown	USA	2
	Yves Tavernier	FRA	2
	Joakim Wallner	SWE	2
101	Ivano Camozzi	ITA	1
	Philippe Verneret	FRA	1
	Klaus Gattermann	BRD	1
	Andy Luhn	USA	1
	Watary Mizutani	JPN	1

WOMEN'S OVERALL 1983

1	Tamara McKinney	USA	225
2	Hanni Wenzel	LIE	193
3	Erika Hess	SUI	192
4	Elisabeth Kirchler	AUT	163
5	Maria Walliser	SUI	135
6	Irene Epple	BRD	117
7	Cindy Nelson	USA	115
8	Olga Charvatova	TCH	111
9	Maria Epple	BRD	108
10	Doris de Agostini	SUI	96
11	Anni Kronbichler	AUT	93
12	Christine Cooper	USA	87
13	Fabienne Serrat	FRA	86
14	Maria Rosa Quario	ITA	82
15	Michaela Gerg	BRD	70
16	Perrine Pelen	FRA	69
17	Elisabeth Chaud	FRA	67
18	Laurie Graham	CAN	66
19	Petra Wenzel	LIE	65
20	Anne-Flore Rey	FRA	63
21	Caroline Attia	FRA	62
22	Malgorzata Tlalka	POL	61
23	Roswitha Steiner	AUT	60
24	Sylvia Eder	AUT	55
25	Zoe Haas	SUI	53
26	Daniela Zini	ITA	52
	Michela Figini	SUI	52
28	Dorota Tlalka	POL	50
29	Jana Gantnerova-Soltysova	TCH	48
30	Claudine Emonet	FRA	44
	Ursula Konzett	LIE	44
32	Lea Soelkner	AUT	42
33	Debbie Armstrong	USA	41
	Heidi Wiesler	BRD	41
35	Monika Hess	SUI	38
	Brigitte Oertli	SUI	38
37	Ariane Ehrat	SUI	37
38	Carole Merle	FRA	35
39	Veronika Vitzthum	AUT	34
	Marie-Luce Waldmeier	FRA	34
	Gerry Sorensen	CAN	34
	Paoletta Magoni	ITA	34
43	Catherine Quittet	FRA	33
44	Hélène Barbier	FRA	28
45	Sieglinde Winkler	AUT	27
46	Lorena Frigo	ITA	23
47	Katrin Gutensohn	AUT	21
48	Maria Maricich	USA	20
49	Anja Zavadlav	JUG	16
	Sigrid Wolf	AUT	16
51	Blanca Fernandez	SPA	15
	Claudia Riedl	AUT	15
53	Françoise Bozon	FRA	13
54	Ivona Valesova	TCH	11
	Sonja Stotz	BRD	11
	Holly Beth Flanders	USA	11
57	Karen Stemmle	CAN	10
58	Karin Buder	AUT	9
	Alexandra Marasova	TCH	9
	Ewa Grabowska	POL	9
	Elena Medzihradska	TCH	9
	Pam Ann Fletcher	USA	9
	Brigitte Nansoz	SUI	9
64	Rosi Aschenwald	AUT	7
65	Heidi Preuss	USA	6
66	Christa Kinshofer	BRD	5
	Marina Kiehl	BRD	5
	Eva Twardokens	USA	5
	Huberta Wolf	AUT	5
	Fulvia Stevenin	ITA	5
	Paola Toniolli	ITA	5
72	Ida Ladstaetter	AUT	4
	Veronique Robin	SUI	4
	Elizabeth Warter	AUT	4
75	Andreja Leskovsek	JUG	3
	Myriam Difant	FRA	3
	Liisa Savijarvi	CAN	3
	Diana Haight	CAN	3
79	Regine Moesenlechner	BRD	1
	Renate Lazak	BRD	1

American double: World Cup winners Phil Mahre and Tamara McKinney

NATIONS' CUP 1983

1	Switzerland	1887
2	Austria	1539
3	USA	978
4	France	690
5	Italy	569
6	Liechtenstein	554
7	Sweden	463
8	West Germany	430
9	Canada	326
10	Yugoslavia	283
11	Czechoslovakia	200
12	Luxembourg	168
13	Poland	120
14	Bulgaria	33
15	USSR	28
16	Norway	25
17	Australia	22
18	Spain	15
19	Hungary	11
20	Japan	10
21	Great Britain	7
22	Denmark	6
	Mexico	6

MEN

1	Switzerland	1215
2	Austria	966
3	Sweden	463
4	USA	440
5	Italy	364
6	Yugoslavia	264
7	Liechtenstein	226
8	Canada	210
9	Luxembourg	168
10	France	116
11	West Germany	58
12	Bulgaria	33
13	USSR	28
14	Norway	25
15	Australia	22
16	Hungary	11
17	Japan	10
18	Czechoslovakia	8
19	Great Britain	7
20	Denmark	6
	Mexico	6

WOMEN

1	Switzerland	672
2	France	574
3	Austria	573
4	USA	538
5	West Germany	372
6	Liechtenstein	328
7	Italy	205
8	Czechoslovakia	192
9	Poland	120
10	Canada	116
11	Yugoslavia	19
12	Spain	15

WORLD CUP RESULTS 1982–3

MEN/DOWNHILL

1983

1	F Klammer	AUT	95
2	C Cathomen	SUI	92
3	H Weirather	AUT	74
4	E Resch	AUT	73
5	P Luescher	SUI	72
	U Raeber	SUI	72
7	P Mueller	SUI	71
8	K Read	CAN	69
9	T Brooker	CAN	67
10	H Hoeflehner	AUT	65
11	S Podborski	CAN	63
12	S Meli	SUI	56
13	B Kernen	SUI	55
14	M Mair	ITA	48
15	L Stock	AUT	41
16	G Pfaffenbichler	AUT	40
17	P Wirnsberger	AUT	32
18	Ph Mahre	USA	28
19	F Heinzer	SUI	23
20	V Makeev	SOV	19
21	D Sbardellotto	ITA	16
	F Stoelzl	AUT	16
23	T Buergler	SUI	15
24	S Niederseer	AUT	13
25	B Flaschberger	AUT	12
26	P Zurbriggen	SUI	11
27	U Spiess	AUT	10
	B Johnson	USA	10
29	S Wildgruber	BRD	9
30	A Wenzel	LIE	7
31	S Lee	AUS	6
32	P Duerr	BRD	5
33	R McLeish	CAN	4
34	M Brown	USA	2
35	P Verneret	FRA	1
	K Gattermann	BRD	1

Pontresina/St Moritz Switzerland
5.12.82

1	Weirather	AUT	1:42.13
2	Klammer	AUT	1:43.15
3	Mueller	SUI	1:43.21
4	Cathomen	SUI	1:43.28
5	Hoeflehner	AUT	1:43.36
6	Read	CAN	1:43.44
7	Wirnsberger	AUT	1:43.57
8	Makeev	SOV	1:43.59
9	T Buergler	SUI	1:43.64
10	Raeber	SUI	1:43.95
11	Meli	SUI	1:44.02
12	Podborski	CAN	1:44.12
13	Kernen	SUI	1:44.14
14	Heinzer	SUI	1:44.18
15	Sbardellotto	ITA	1:44.20

High hatting it: Franz Klammer celebrates his downhill triumph at Lake Louise

Val Gardena Italy
19.12.82

1	Cathomen	SUI	2:09.54
2	Resch	AUT	2:09.87
3	Klammer	AUT	2:10.09
4	Raeber	SUI	2:10.12
5	Read	CAN	2:10.39
6	Weirather	AUT	2:10.69
7	Heinzer	SUI	2:10.71
8	Stock	AUT	2:10.79
9	Hoeflehner	AUT	2:10.81
10	Wirnsberger	AUT	2:11.11
11	Brooker	CAN	2:11.35
12	Flaschberger	AUT	2:11.47
13	Niederseer	AUT	2:11.64
14	Mair	ITA	2:11.72
15	Gattermann	BRD	2:11.87

Val Gardena Italy
20.12.82

1	Klammer	AUT	2:08.91
2	Mueller	SUI	2:09.39
3	Raeber	SUI	2:09.61
4	Heinzer	SUI	2:09.64
5	Weirather	AUT	2:10.32
6	Brooker	CAN	2:10.58
7	Read	CAN	2:10.61
8	Stock	AUT	2:11.06
9	Cathomen	SUI	2:11.07
10	Kernen	SUI	2:11.30
11	Flaschberger	AUT	2:11.46
12	Hoeflehner	AUT	2:11.47
13	Wirnsberger	AUT	2:11.59
14	Niederseer	AUT	2:11.72
15	Makeev	SOV	2:11.80

Val d'isère France
9.1.83

1	Resch	AUT	1:59.26
2	Luescher	SUI	1:59.44
3	Cathomen	SUI	1:59.56
4	Read	CAN	1:59.57
5	Mair	ITA	1:59.64
6	Weirather	AUT	1:59.71
7	Meli	SUI	1:59.87
8	Stoelzl	AUT	1:59.93
9	Raeber	AUT	2:00.00
10	Stock	AUT	2:00.44
11	Duerr	BRD	2:00.46
12	Klammer	AUT	2:00.61
13	Flaschberger	AUT	2:00.64
14	Ph Mahre	USA	2:00.80
15	Makeev	SOV	2:00.85

Val d'Isère France
10.1.83

1	Cathomen	SUI	1:59.20

2	Read	CAN	1:59.32
3	Sbardellotto	ITA	1:59.66
4	Mueller	SUI	1:59.73
5	Klammer	AUT	1:59.75
6	Raeber	SUI	1:59.81
7	Kernen	SUI	1:59.91
8	Stoelzl	AUT	2:00.00
9	Meli	SUI	2:00.08
10	Makeev	SOV	2:00.09
11	Hoeflehner	AUT	2:00.11
12	Stock	AUT	2:00.31
13	Mair	ITA	2:00.33
14	Niederseer	AUT	2:00.38
	T Buergler	SUI	2:00.38

Kitzbuehel Austria
21.1.83

1	Kernen	SUI	2:06.68
2	Podborski	CAN	2:06.79
3	Raeber	SUI	2:07.10
4	Mueller	SUI	2:07.32
5	Weirather	AUT	2:07.39
6	Spiess	AUT	2:07.90
7	Luescher	AUT	2:07.93
8	Meli	SUI	2:07.97
9	Zurbriggen	SUI	2:08.06
10	Lee	AUS	2:08.23
	Hoeflehner	AUT	2:08.23
12	Ph Mahre	USA	2:08.31
13	McLeish	CAN	2:08.41
	Read	CAN	2:08.41
15	Verneret	FRA	2:08.48

Kitzbuehel Austria
22.1.83

1	Brooker	CAN	2:01.96
2	Raeber	SUI	2:02.19
3	Read	CAN	2:02.47
4	Mueller	SUI	2:02.69
	Meli	SUI	2:02.69
6	Klammer	AUT	2:02.79
7	Kernen	SUI	2:02.97
8	Luescher	SUI	2:03.05
9	Podborski	CAN	2:03.20
10	Wirnsberger	AUT	2:03.23
11	Weirather	AUT	2:03.45
12	Stock	AUT	2:03.57
13	Ph Mahre	USA	2:03.58
14	Resch	AUT	2:03.72
15	Cathomen	SUI	2:03.80

Sarajevo Yugoslavia
28.1.83

1	Pfaffenbichler	AUT	1:48.81
2	Podborski	CAN	1:49.02
3	Klammer	AUT	1:49.07
4	Mair	ITA	1:49.66
5	Read	CAN	1:49.76
6	Luescher	SUI	1:50.03
7	Raeber	SUI	1:50.07
8	Wildgruber	BRD	1:50.27
9	Hoflehner	AUT	1:50.30
10	Meli	SUI	1:50.31
11	Weirather	AUT	1:50.58
12	Niederseer	AUT	1:50.83
13	Resch	AUT	1:50.88
14	Brooker	CAN	1:50.94
15	Kernen	SUI	1:51.21

First-time winner: Bruno Kernen (*left*) edges out downhill title-holder Steve Podborski at Kitzbuehel

St Anton Austria
5.2.83

1	Luescher	SUI	2:04.22
2	Meli	SUI	2:04.82
3	Weirather	AUT	2:05.00
4	Podborski	CAN	2:05.08
5	Ph Mahre	USA	2:05.19
6	Johnson	USA	2:05.50
7	Stock	AUT	2:05.53
8	Klammer	AUT	2:05.67
9	Wenzel	LIE	2:05.78
10	T Buergler	SUI	2:06.18
11	Resch	AUT	2:06.20
12	Zurbriggen	SUI	2:06.22
13	Makeev	SOV	2:06.30
14	Hoeflehner	AUT	2:06.39
15	Brooker	CAN	2:06.40

Aspen USA
6.3.83

1	Brooker	CAN	1:47.87
2	Mair	ITA	1:48.24
3	Hoeflehner	AUT	1:48.54
4	Weirather	AUT	1:48.68
5	Resch	AUT	1:48.76

6	Mueller	SUI	1:48.82
7	Raeber	SUI	1:48.87
8	Cathomen	SUI	1:48.97
9	Ph Mahre	USA	1:49.08
10	Pfaffenbichler	AUT	1:49.17
11	Read	CAN	1:49.38
12	Kernen	SUI	1:49.40
13	Klammer	AUT	1:49.42
14	Brown	USA	1:49.46
15	Wildgruber	BRD	1:49.48

Boost for Canada: Todd Brooker chaired by Helmut Hoeflehner (*left*) and Michael Mair after Aspen

Lake Louise Canada
12.3.83

1	Hoeflehner	AUT	1:40.52
2	Klammer	AUT	1:40.75
3	Cathomen	SUI	1:40.77
4	Resch	AUT	1:40.82
	Mueller	SUI	1:40.82
6	Stock	AUT	1:41.02
7	Pfaffenbichler	AUT	1:41.05
8	Wirnsberger	AUT	1:41.09
9	Raeber	SUI	1:41.11
10	Kernen	SUI	1:41.17
11	Weirather	AUT	1:41.26
12	Meli	SUI	1:41.41
13	Ph Mahre	USA	1:41.44
14	Niederseer	AUT	1:41.62
15	McLeish	CAN	1:41.68

Second but still winner: Klammer (*left*) clinches the downhill title at Lake Louise. Hoeflehner (*centre*) wins, Cathomen is third

MEN/SLALOM

1983

1	I Stenmark	SWE	110
	S Strand	SWE	110
3	A Wenzel	LIE	92
4	S Mahre	USA	80
5	B Krizaj	JUG	78
6	Ph Mahre	USA	75
7	M Girardelli	LUX	69
8	P de Chiesa	ITA	67
9	F Gruber	AUT	66
10	C Orlainsky	AUT	62
11	M Canac	FRA	52
12	B Fjaellberg	SWE	49
13	J. Luethy	SUI	42
14	I Edalini	ITA	34
	P Frommelt	LIE	34
16	P Popangelov	BUL	33
17	L Halvarsson	SWE	27
18	K Heidegger	AUT	23
19	J Kuralt	JUG	22
20	A Giorgi	ITA	20
21	P Zurbriggen	SUI	13
	M Julen	SUI	13
23	F Woerndl	BRD	12
24	P Mally	ITA	11
25	H Pieren	SUI	10
	M Vion	FRA	10
27	D Bouvet	FRA	9
	D Fontaine	FRA	9
29	H Gstrein	AUT	8
	P A Skajem	NOR	8
	J Sunqvist	SWE	8
32	M Tonazzi	ITA	7
33	D Mougel	FRA	6
	F Beck	BRD	6
	R Erlacher	ITA	6
	J Franko	JUG	6
37	O Soerli	NOR	5
38	H Spiss	AUT	4
	J Gaspoz	SUI	4
	N Iwaya	JPN	4
41	V Andreev	SOV	3
	T Cerkovnik	JUG	3
	H Ohtaka	JPN	3
44	T Kaiwa	JPN	2
	O Totsch	ITA	2
	J Wallner	SWE	2
47	W Mizutani	JPN	1
	Y Tavernier	FRA	1

Courmayeur Italy
14.12.82

1	Stenmark	SWE	1:42.12
2	Strand	SWE	1:42.43
3	Ph Mahre	USA	1:42.86
4	S Mahre	USA	1:43.36
5	Krizaj	JUG	1:43.90
6	Orlainsky	AUT	1:44.39
7	de Chiesa	ITA	1:44.46
8	Zurbriggen	SUI	1:45.35
9	Julen	SUI	1:46.26

Friends and neighbours: Stig Strand (*right*) wins Madonna's slalom. Ingemar Stenmark, also from Tarnaby, is second

10	Girardelli	LUX	1:46.28
11	Halvarsson	SWE	1:46.30
12	Mally	ITA	1:46.48
13	Edalini	ITA	1:46.63
14	Luethy	SUI	1:46.66
15	Fjaellberg	SWE	1:46.68

Madonna di Campiglio Italy
21.12.82

1	Strand	SWE	1:38.99
2	Stenmark	SWE	1:39.23
3	Ph Mahre	USA	1:39.26
4	Krizaj	JUG	1:39.37
5	de Chiesa	ITA	1:39.44
6	Orlainsky	AUT	1:39.64
7	Gruber	AUT	1:40.52
8	S Mahre	USA	1:40.59
9	Canac	FRA	1:40.75
10	Edalini	ITA	1:40.84
11	Zurbriggen	SUI	1:40.89
12	Popangelov	BUL	1:41.51
13	Halvarsson	SWE	1:41.96
14	Luethy	SUI	1:42.27
15	Andreev	SOV	1:42.59

Parpan Switzerland
4.1.83

1	S Mahre	USA	1:38.96
2	Luethy	SUI	1:40.73
3	Wenzel	LIE	1:40.92
4	de Chiesa	ITA	1:41.27
5	Gruber	AUT	1:41.38
6	Pieren	SUI	1:41.52
7	Canac	FRA	1:41.99
8	Woerndl	BRD	1:42.23
9	Tonazzi	ITA	1:42.28
10	Julen	SUI	1:42.33
11	Heidegger	AUT	1:43.00
12	Franko	JUG	1:43.15
13	Mougel	FRA	1:43.41
14	Andreev	SOV	1:43.46
	Kaiwa	JPN	1:43.46

Kitzbuehel Austria
23.1.83

1	Stenmark	SWE	1:45.43
2	Orlainsky	AUT	1:46.37
3	Ph Mahre	USA	1:46.56
4	Girardelli	LUX	1:46.98
5	de Chiesa	ITA	1:47.71
6	S Mahre	USA	1:48.31
7	Strand	SWE	1:48.35
8	Fontaine	FRA	1:48.58
9	Canac	FRA	1:48.80
10	Popangelov	BUL	1:49.01
11	Vion	FRA	1:49.09
12	Fjaellberg	SWE	1:49.27
13	Mougel	FRA	1:49.32
14	Bouvet	FRA	1:49.37
15	Cerkovnik	JUG	1:49.38

Kranjska Gora Yugoslavia
30.1.83

1	Gruber	AUT	1:28.62
2	Strand	SWE	1:28.96
3	Canac	FRA	1:29.43
4	de Chiesa	ITA	1:29.77
5	Frommelt	LIE	1:30.14
6	Halvarsson	SWE	1:31.42
7	Heidegger	AUT	1:31.62
8	Gstrein	AUT	1:31.71
9	Bouvet	FRA	1:32.03
10	Beck	BRD	1:32.14
11	Popangelov	BUL	1:32.23
12	Spiss	AUT	1:32.29
13	Giorgi	ITA	1:32.30
14	Skajem	NOR	1:32.40
15	Cerkovnik	JUG	1:33.14

St Anton Austria
6.2.83

1	S Mahre	USA	1:51.44
2	Wenzel	LIE	1:51.49
3	Ph Mahre	USA	1:51.61
4	Canac	FRA	1:51.82
5	Edalini	ITA	1:52.06
6	Frommelt	LIE	1:52.27
7	Girardelli	LUX	1:52.87
8	Fjaellberg	SWE	1:52.94
9	Popangelov	BUL	1:53.24
10	Gruber	AUT	1:53.27
11	Soerli	NOR	1:53.45
12	Woerndl	BRD	1:53.53
13	Kuralt	JUG	1:53.73
14	Luethy	SUI	1:53.78
15	Skajem	NOR	1:54.09

Markstein France
11.2.83

1	Stenmark	SWE	1:44.54
2	de Chiesa	ITA	1:45.04
3	Ph Mahre	USA	1:45.23
4	Wenzel	LIE	1:45.38
5	Girardelli	LUX	1:45.52
6	Luethy	SUI	1:45.86
7	Gruber	AUT	1:45.94
8	Fjaellberg	SWE	1:46.00
9	Frommelt	LIE	1:46.13
10	Krizaj	JUG	1:46.15
11	S Mahre	USA	1:46.19
12	Heidegger	AUT	1:46.34
13	Strand	SWE	1:46.53
14	Giorgi	ITA	1:46.69
15	Kuralt	JUG	1:46.75

Markstein France
12.2.83

1	Krizaj	JUG	1:38.98
2	Fjaellberg	SWE	1:39.42
3	Orlainsky	AUT	1:39.56
4	Strand	SWE	1:39.67
5	Ph Mahre	USA	1:39.70
6	Stenmark	SWE	1:39.73
7	Wenzel	LIE	1:39.85
8	Luethy	SUI	1:40.09
9	Kuralt	JUG	1:40.63
10	Popangelov	BUL	1:40.70
11	Heidegger	AUT	1:40.79
12	Halvarsson	SWE	1:40.80
13	Canac	FRA	1:40.82
14	Totsch	ITA	1:40.95
15	Fontaine	FRA	1:40.97

Three's company: Phil Mahre (*right*) is third for the fourth time in the St Anton slalom. Steve Mahre (*centre*) wins, Wenzel is second

Tarnaby Sweden
23.2.83

1	Wenzel	LIE	1:40.48
2	Strand	SWE	1:40.98
3	Krizaj	JUG	1:41.20
4	Girardelli	LUX	1:41.52
5	Edalini	ITA	1:41.78
6	Gruber	AUT	1:41.91
7	Popangelov	BUL	1:42.13
8	de Chiesa	ITA	1:42.15
9	Giorgi	ITA	1:42.78
10	Frommelt	LIE	1:43.15
11	Skajem	NOR	1:43.50
	Mally	ITA	1:43.50
	Vion	FRA	1:43.50
14	Wallner	SWE	1:44.08
15	Cerkovnik	JUG	1:44.09

Gällivare Sweden
27.2.83

1	Girardelli	LUX	1:32.49
2	Strand	SWE	1:33.88
3	Stenmark	SWE	1:34.08
4	Ph Mahre	USA	1:34.47
5	Krizaj	JUG	1:35.03
6	de Chiesa	ITA	1:35.35
7	Fjaellberg	SWE	1:35.37
8	Sundqvist	SWE	1:35.53
9	Gruber	AUT	1:36.47
10	Kuralt	JUG	1:36.62
11	Halvarsson	SWE	1:36.76
12	Gaspoz	SUI	1:37.19
13	Edalini	ITA	1:37.24
14	Mally	ITA	1:37.79
15	Tavernier	FRA	1:38.31

Furano Japan
20.3.83

1	Strand	SWE	1:32.31
2	Wenzel	LIE	1:32.82
3	Krizaj	JUG	1:33.82
4	de Chiesa	ITA	1:33.67
5	Gruber	AUT	1:34.39
6	Ph Mahre	USA	1:34.49
7	Canac	FRA	1:35.36
8	Giorgi	ITA	1:35.94
9	Orlainsky	AUT	1:35.97
10	Erlacher	ITA	1:36.23
11	Kuralt	JUG	1:37.18
12	Iwaya	JPN	1:37.86
13	Ohtaka	JPN	1:38.68
14	Franko	JUG	1:39.64
15	Mizutani	JPN	1:39.73

MEN/SUPER AND GIANT SLALOM

1983

1	Ph Mahre	USA	107
2	M Julen	SUI	100
	I Stenmark	SWE	100
4	P Zurbriggen	SUI	90
5	H Enn	AUT	83
6	M Girardelli	LUX	52
7	P Luescher	SUI	51
8	R Erlacher	ITA	50
	J Franko	JUG	50
10	J Luethy	SUI	44
11	B Strel	JUG	43
12	A Wenzel	LIE	38
13	Th Buergler	SUI	36
14	F Gruber	AUT	31
15	A Giorgi	ITA	27
	P Mueller	SUI	27
	H Strolz	AUT	27
18	M Mair	ITA	25
19	F Heinzer	SUI	24
20	B Krizaj	JUG	22
21	G Benedik	SWE	21
22	S Kerschbaumer	ITA	19
23	C Orlainsky	AUT	17
24	H Weirather	AUT	16
25	G Mader	AUT	15
26	L Stock	AUT	14
27	S Mahre	USA	13
28	J Wallner	SWE	12
29	E Hirt	BRD	11
	O Soerli	NOR	11
31	P Lamotte	FRA	10
	F Woerndl	BRD	10
33	H Pieren	SUI	8
34	T Jakobsson	SWE	5
	H Spiss	AUT	5
	J Sundqvist	SWE	5
37	J Gaspoz	SUI	3
38	M Hangl	SUI	2
	G Hinterseer	AUT	2
40	Y Camozzi	ITA	1
	Y Tavernier	FRA	1

Val d'Isère France
12.12.82 Super

1	Mueller	SUI	1:35.16
2	Luescher	SUI	1:35.22
3	Zurbriggen	SUI	1:35.77
4	Heinzer	SUI	1:36.03
5	Th Buergler	SUI	1:36.26
6	Enn	AUT	1:36.51
7	Franko	JUG	1:36.52
8	Weirather	AUT	1:36.59
9	Krizaj	JUG	1:36.61
10	Orlainsky	AUT	1:36.79
11	Strolz	AUT	1:36.83
12	Erlacher	ITA	1:36.87
13	Kerschbaumer	ITA	1:36.90
14	Wenzel	LIE	1:36.92
	Hangl	SUI	1:36.92

Madonna di Campiglio Italy
22.12.82 Super

1	Mair	ITA	1:43.71
2	Enn	AUT	1:43.86
3	Zurbriggen	SUI	1:43.95
4	Heinzer	SUI	1:43.97
5	Strolz	AUT	1:44.24
6	Franko	JUG	1:44.47
7	Mader	AUT	1:44.49
8	Weirather	AUT	1:44.70
9	Benedik	JUG	1:44.73
10	Kerschbaumer	ITA	1:44.83
11	Erlacher	ITA	1:44.86
12	Stock	AUT	1:45.04
13	Gruber	AUT	1:45.12
14	Luescher	SUI	1:45.16
15	Wenzel	LIE	1:45.21

Adelboden Switzerland
11.1.83

1	Zurbriggen	SUI	2:24.94
2	Julen	SUI	2:25.19
3	Luethy	SUI	2:25.92
4	Krizaj	JUG	2:26.01
5	Franko	JUG	2:26.18
6	Wenzel	LIE	2:26.20
7	Girardelli	LUX	2:26.31
	Stenmark	SWE	2:26.31
9	Th Buergler	SUI	2:26.67
10	Pieren	SUI	2:26.88
11	Ph Mahre	USA	2:27.18
12	Enn	AUT	2:27.65
13	Jakobsson	SWE	2:28.74
14	Spiss	AUT	2:28.84
15	Camozzi	ITA	2:29.02
	Benedik	JUG	2:29.02
	Giorgi	ITA	2:29.02

Kranjska Gora Yugoslavia
29.1.83

1	Enn	AUT	2:24.19
2	Julen	SUI	2:24.45
3	Stenmark	SWE	2:24.89
4	Erlacher	ITA	2:24.93
5	Ph Mahre	USA	2:25.16
6	Giorgi	ITA	2:25.25
7	Luethy	SUI	2:25.62
8	Th Buergler	SUI	2:25.88
9	Franko	JUG	2:25.90
10	Girardelli	LUX	2:26.32
11	Strel	JUG	2:26.51
12	Zurbriggen	SUI	2:26.53
13	Krizaj	JUG	2:26.54
14	Orlainsky	AUT	2:26.69
15	Wenzel	LIE	2:26.84

Garmisch-Partenkirchen
West Germany Super
9.2.83

1	Luescher	SUI	1:36.45
2	Zurbriggen	SUI	1:36.65
3	Enn	AUT	1:37.60
4	Wenzel	LIE	1:37.88
5	Strolz	AUT	1:37.89
6	Kerschbaumer	ITA	1:37.93
7	Luethy	SUI	1:37.97
8	Franko	JUG	1:38.22
9	Girardelli	LUX	1:38.24
10	Erlacher	ITA	1:38.35
11	Stenmark	SWE	1:38.82
	Strel	JUG	1:38.82
13	Julen	SUI	1:38.91
14	Orlainsky	AUT	1:38.98
15	Benedik	JUG	1:39.05

Super Peter: Switzerland's one-time Peter 'Loser' Luescher, first in the Garmisch Super G from Pirmin Zurbriggen (*right*) and Hans Enn

Todtnau Switzerland
13.2.83

1	Stenmark	SWE	2:45.66
2	Julen	SUI	2:46.68
3	Zurbriggen	SUI	2:46.71
4	Ph Mahre	USA	2:46.76
5	Wenzel	LIE	2:47.11
6	Strel	JUG	2:48.01
	Girardelli	LUX	2:48.01
8	Erlacher	ITA	2:48.37
9	Hirt	BRD	2:48.39
10	Lamotte	FRA	2:48.76
11	Gruber	AUT	2:49.24
12	Orlainsky	AUT	2:49.48
13	Gaspoz	SUI	2:49.51
14	Woerndl	BRD	2:49.61
15	Th Buergler	SUI	2:49.84

Gällivare Sweden
26.2.83

1	Stenmark	SWE	2:29.11
2	Julen	SUI	2:30.83
	Ph Mahre	USA	2:30.83
4	Wallner	SWE	2:30.88
5	Strel	JUG	2:31.04
6	Luethy	SUI	2:31.08
7	Franko	JUG	2:31.27
8	Gruber	AUT	2:31.43
9	Zurbriggen	SUI	2:31.47
10	Benedik	JUG	2:31.53
11	Sundqvist	SWE	2:31.69
12	Soerli	NOR	2:31.93
13	Spiss	AUT	2:31.94
14	Pieren	SUI	2:32.18
	Jakobsson	SWE	2:32.18

Aspen USA
7.3.83

1	Ph Mahre	USA	2:31.49
2	Girardelli	LUX	2:31.73
3	Stenmark	SWE	2:32.09
4	Julen	SUI	2:32.65
5	Franko	JUG	2:32.69
6	Giorgi	ITA	2:33.06
7	Erlacher	ITA	2:33.17
8	Zurbriggen	SUI	2:33.59
9	Enn	AUT	2:34.52
10	Mader	AUT	2:34.53
11	S Mahre	USA	2:34.69
12	Hirt	BRD	2:34.81
13	Wenzel	LIE	2:34.92
14	Soerli	NOR	2:35.06
15	Luethy	SUI	2:35.11

Vail USA
8.3.83

1	Ph Mahre	USA	3:03.00
2	Stenmark	SWE	3:03.14
3	Julen	SUI	3:03.52
4	Erlacher	ITA	3:04.01
5	Enn	AUT	3:04.29
6	Gruber	AUT	3:04.33
7	Th Buergler	SUI	3:04.47
8	S Mahre	USA	3:04.51
9	Strel	JUG	3:04.52
10	Giorgi	ITA	3:05.27
11	Soerli	NOR	3:05.95
12	Lamotte	FRA	3:06.21
13	Stock	AUT	3:06.22
14	Hinterseer	AUT	3:06.87
15	Tavernier	FRA	3:06.99

Furano Japan
19.3.83

1	Ph Mahre	USA	2:35.20
2	Julen	SUI	2:35.21
3	Stenmark	SWE	2:35.27
4	Enn	AUT	2:35.55
5	Zurbriggen	SUI	2:35.72
6	Strel	JUG	2:36.13
7	Erlacher	ITA	2:36.59
8	Woerndl	BRD	2:36.78
9	Stock	AUT	2:37.13
10	Benedik	JUG	2:37.16
11	Gruber	AUT	2:37.23
12	Luescher	SUI	2:37.30
13	Orlainsky	AUT	2:37.35
14	Mueller	SUI	2:37.48
15	Franko	JUG	2:37.70

MEN/COMBINED

Val d'Isère/Val Gardena

1	Heinzer	SUI
2	Mueller	SUI
3	Luescher	SUI
4	Weirather	AUT
5	Raeber	SUI
6	Zurbriggen	SUI
7	Hoeflehner	AUT
8	Cathomen	SUI
9	Read	CAN
10	Sbardellotto	ITA
11	Mair	ITA
12	Makeev	SOV
13	Hinterseer	AUT
14	Cochrane	USA
15	Luhn	USA

Madonna di Campiglio

1	Zurbriggen	SUI
2	Orlainsky	AUT
3	Gruber	AUT
4	Krizaj	JUG
5	Strolz	AUT
6	Luethy	SUI
7	Erlacher	ITA
8	Stenmark	SWE
9	Canac	FRA
10	Spiss	AUT
11	Edalini	ITA
12	Woerndl	BRD
13	Julen	SUI
14	Andreev	SOV
15	Enn	AUT

Kitzbuehel

1	Ph Mahre	USA
2	Girardelli	LUX
3	Luescher	SUI
4	Kernen	SUI
5	Meli	SUI
6	Fahner	SUI
7	Raeber	SUI
8	Soltys	TCH
9	Mueller	SUI
10	Gotzy	HUN
11	Voelgyesi	HUN

Kitzbuehel/Markstein

1	Ph Mahre	USA
2	Wenzel	LIE
3	Girardelli	LUX
4	Zurbriggen	SUI
5	Luescher	SUI
6	Kernen	SUI
7	Meli	SUI
8	Lee	AUS
9	Raeber	SUI
10	von Hohenlohe	MEX

St Anton

1	Ph Mahre	USA
2	Wenzel	LIE
3	S Mahre	USA
4	Girardelli	LUX
5	Luescher	SUI
6	Rambaud	FRA
7	Meli	SUI
8	Lee	AUS
9	Bell	GBR
10	Boedker	DAN

WOMEN/DOWNHILL

1983

1	D de Agostini	SUI	106
2	M Walliser	SUI	97
3	E Kirchler	AUT	76
4	C Attia	FRA	66
5	L Graham	CAN	63
6	E Chaud	FRA	50
7	J. Gantnerova-Soltysova	TCH	47
8	C Emonet	FRA	44
9	L Soelkner	AUT	40
10	A Ehrat	SUI	39
11	G Sorensen	CAN	36
	V Vitzthum	AUT	36
13	M L Waldmeier	FRA	34
14	C Quittet	FRA	29
15	S Winkler	AUT	27
16	S Eder	AUT	26
	M Gerg	BRD	26
18	I Epple	BRD	24
19	D Armstrong	USA	22
20	M Maricich	USA	20
	O Charvatova	TCH	20
22	H Wiesler	BRD	17
23	S Wolf	AUT	16
24	M Figini	SUI	15
25	C Nelson	USA	13
26	B Oertli	SUI	11
	H Flanders	USA	11
	F Bozon	FRA	11
29	K Stemmle	CAN	10
30	P A Fletcher	USA	9
31	C Merle	FRA	6
32	H Wolf	BRD	5
33	E Warter	AUT	4
34	L Savijarvi	CAN	3
	D Haight	CAN	3
	K Gutensohn	AUT	3
37	Z Haas	SUI	2
	S Stotz	BRD	2
39	R Moesenlechner	BRD	1

Val d'Isère France
7.12.82

1	de Agostini	SUI	1:22.58
2	Soelkner	AUT	1:22.96
3	Walliser	SUI	1:23.61
4	Sorensen	CAN	1:23.88
5	Chaud	FRA	1:23.90
6	Kirchler	AUT	1:23.93
	Graham	CAN	1:23.93
8	Eder	AUT	1:23.95
	Waldmeier	FRA	1:23.95
10	I Epple	BRD	1:23.99
11	H Wolf	AUT	1:24.30
12	Attia	FRA	1:24.32
13	Haight	CAN	1:24.42
14	Haas	SUI	1:24.48
15	Nelson	USA	1:24.67

Sansicario Italy
15.12.82

1	Attia	FRA	1:24.57
2	Emonet	FRA	1:24.86
3	Wiesler	BRD	1:25.16
4	Quittet	FRA	1:25.59
5	Bozon	FRA	1:25.68
6	Gantnerova-Soltysova	TCH	1:25.74
7	Armstrong	USA	1:25.83

Swiss rolling: Doris de Agostini (*right*) wins the downhill title from Maria Walliser

Vive la France: Caroline Attia wins Sansicario from Claudine Emonet (*left*). Fabienne Serrat and Perrine Pelen join the celebrations

8	Ehrat	SUI	1:25.84
9	Oertli	SUI	1:25.89
10	Winkler	AUT	1:25.91
11	Graham	CAN	1:26.11
12	Waldmeier	FRA	1:26.28
	I Epple	BRD	1:26.28
14	Vitzthum	AUT	1:26.31
15	de Agostini	SUI	1:26.41

Schruns/Tschagguns Austria
14.1.83

1	de Agostini	SUI	1:24.57
2	Chaud	FRA	1:24.69
3	Attia	FRA	1:24.89
4	Graham	CAN	1:25.08
5	Sorensen	CAN	1:25.12
6	I Epple	BRD	1:25.30
7	Gantnerova-Soltysova	TCH	1:25.32
8	Walliser	SUI	1:25.37
9	Waldmeier	FRA	1:25.49
10	Vitzthum	AUT	1:25.59
11	Ehrat	SUI	1:25.64
12	Gerg	BRD	1:25.66
13	Gutensohn	AUT	1:25.70
14	Wiesler	BRD	1:25.71
15	Kirchler	AUT	1:25.72

Megève/St Gervais France
21.1.83

1	Walliser	SUI	1:24.52
2	Maricich	USA	1:24.71
3	Waldmeier	FRA	1:24.78
4	Gerg	BRD	1:25.04
5	Gantnerova-Soltysova	TCH	1:25.08
6	de Agostini	SUI	1:25.10
7	Sorensen	CAN	1:25.13
8	Flanders	USA	1:25.17
	Eder	AUT	1:25.17
10	Merle	FRA	1:25.19
11	Vitzthum	AUT	1:25.21
12	I Epple	BRD	1:25.31
13	Chaud	FRA	1:25.34
14	Ehrat	SUI	1:25.41
	Soelkner	AUT	1:25.41

Megève/St Gervais France
22.1.83

1	Kirchler	AUT	1:23.31
2	de Agostini	SUI	1:23.40
3	Attia	FRA	1:23.69
4	Winkler	AUT	1:23.82
5	Emonet	FRA	1:24.00
6	Gantnerova-Soltysova	TCH	1:24.08
7	Gerg	BRD	1:24.11
	Ehrat	SUI	1:24.11
	Soelkner	AUT	1:24.11
10	Walliser	SUI	1:24.13
11	Quittet	FRA	1:24.21
12	Graham	CAN	1:24.24
13	Chaud	FRA	1:24.25
14	Stotz	BRD	1:24.29
15	Eder	AUT	1:24.30

Les Diablerets Switzerland
29.1.83

1	de Agostini	SUI	1:24.65
2	Kirchler	AUT	1:25.13
3	Vitzthum	AUT	1:25.44
4	Walliser	SUI	1:25.91
5	Armstrong	USA	1:26.05
6	S Wolf	AUT	1:26.14
7	Winkler	AUT	1:26.39
8	Eder	AUT	1:26.52
9	Attia	FRA	1:26.00
10	Graham	CAN	1:26.94
11	Chaud	FRA	1:26.95
12	Soelkner	AUT	1:26.96
13	Nelson	USA	1:27.02
14	Sorensen	CAN	1:27.05
15	Gerg	BRD	1:27.06

Sarajevo Yugoslavia
5.2.83

1	Walliser	SUI	1:19.88
2	Kirchler	AUT	1:20.67
3	Ehrat	SUI	1:21.10
4	Charvatova	TCH	1:21.17

Third win for de Agostini . . . but two Austrians, Elisabeth Kirchler (*left*) and Veronika Vitzthum, chased her home

5	Chaud	FRA	1:21.26
6	Graham	CAN	1:21.30
7	Nelson	USA	1:21.31
8	Emonet	FRA	1:21.38
9	Gantnerova-Soltysova	TCH	1:21.40
10	de Agostini	SUI	1:21.41
11	Soelkner	AUT	1:21.45
12	Warter	AUT	1:21.58
13	Flanders	USA	1:21.59
14	Sorensen	CAN	1:21.67
15	Moesenlechner	BRD	1:21.69

Mont Tremblant Canada
5.3.83

1	Graham	CAN	1:32.53
2	Walliser	SUI	1:32.93
3	Figini	SUI	1:33.52
4	Quittet	FRA	1:33.55
5	de Agostini	SUI	1:33.64
6	Stemmle	CAN	1:33.80
7	Fletcher	USA	1:33.92
8	Charvatova	TCH	1:33.94
	Vitzthum	AUT	1:33.94
10	S Wolf	AUT	1:34.11
11	Emonet	FRA	1:34.18
12	Oertli	SUI	1:34.20
13	Savijarvi	CAN	1:34.23
14	Armstrong	USA	1:34.39
15	Eder	AUT	1:34.42

WOMEN/SLALOM

1983

1	E Hess	SUI	110
2	T McKinney	USA	105
3	M R Quario	ITA	89
4	H Wenzel	LIE	82
5	R Steiner	AUT	70
6	A Kronbichler	AUT	66
7	M Tlalka	POL	65
8	D Tlalka	POL	54
9	D Zini	ITA	47
10	P Wenzel	LIE	46
11	P Pelen	FRA	45
12	M Epple	BRD	44
13	P Magoni	ITA	39
14	O Charvatova	TCH	35
15	U Konzett	LIE	31
16	C Cooper	USA	27
17	L Frigo	ITA	23
18	M Hess	SUI	20
19	A Zavadlav	JUG	16
20	F Serrat	FRA	14
21	K Buder	AUT	9
	A Marasova	TCH	9
	B Nansoz	SUI	9
24	H Barbier	FRA	8
	E Grabowska	POL	8
26	R Aschenwald	AUT	7
27	B Fernandez	SPA	6
	A F Rey	FRA	6
29	C Kinshofer	BRD	5
	B Oertli	SUI	5
	P Toniolli	ITA	5
32	I Ladstaetter	AUT	4
	L Soelkner	AUT	4
	F Stevenin	ITA	4
35	M Gerg	BRD	3
	A Leskovsek	JUG	3
	H Preuss	USA	3
38	I Epple	BRD	2
39	S Eder	AUT	1
	R Lazak	BRD	1
	C Nelson	USA	1

Limone Piemonte Italy
10.12.82

1	McKinney	USA	1:36.61
2	E Hess	SUI	1:36.77
3	H Wenzel	LIE	1:37.17
4	Quario	ITA	1:37.40
5	Zini	ITA	1:37.43
6	M Epple	BRD	1:38.51
7	Konzett	LIE	1:39.04
8	Magoni	ITA	1:39.08
9	Kronbichler	AUT	1:39.47
10	Frigo	ITA	1:39.52
11	Zavadlav	JUG	1:39.59
12	Pelen	FRA	1:39.64
13	Leskovsek	JUG	1:39.65
14	Oertli	SUI	1:39.72
15	D Tlalka	POL	1:39.77

Swiss kiss: Erika Hess and Doris de Agostini at Val d'Isère

Piancavallo Italy
17.12.82

1	E Hess	SUI	1:47.04
2	Pelen	FRA	1:47.08
3	Cooper	USA	1:47.91
4	H Wenzel	LIE	1:48.31
5	M Epple	BRD	1:49.10
6	Magoni	ITA	1:49.41
7	Frigo	ITA	1:49.93
8	D Tlalka	POL	1:50.05
9	Quario	ITA	1:50.07
10	Kronbichler	AUT	1:50.14
11	Nansoz	SUI	1:50.93
12	Stevenin	ITA	1:51.09
13	Toniolli	ITA	1:51.19
14	Zavadlav	JUG	1:51.21
15	Serrat	FRA	1:51.38

Waiting on McKinney: Erika Hess and Maria Rosa Quario at Limone

Davos Switzerland
11.1.83

1	McKinney	USA	1:25.26
2	E Hess	SUI	1:25.44
3	Pelen	FRA	1:25.73
4	Cooper	USA	1:25.79
5	H Wenzel	LIE	1:25.82
6	Steiner	AUT	1:25.91
7	P Wenzel	LIE	1:27.26
8	Magoni	ITA	1:27.45
9	M Epple	BRD	1:27.46
10	Buder	AUT	1:27.89
11	Quario	ITA	1:28.31
12	Charvatova	TCH	1:28.60
13	Kronbichler	AUT	1:28.85
14	Toniolli	ITA	1:29.57
15	Lazak	BRD	1:29.72

Schruns/Tschagguns Austria
16.1.83

1	Kronbichler	AUT	1:38.35
2	Quario	ITA	1:38.54
	M Tlalka	POL	1:38.54
4	D Tlalka	POL	1:38.95
5	Steiner	AUT	1:39.07
6	Charvatova	TCH	1:40.23
7	Marasova	TCH	1:40.70
8	Serrat	FRA	1:40.89
9	Aschenwald	AUT	1:41.20
10	M Epple	BRD	1:41.30
11	Frigo	ITA	1:41.63
12	Ladstaetter	AUT	1:41.83
13	P Wenzel	LIE	1:41.92
14	Zavadlav	JUG	1:42.08
15	Eder	AUT	1:42.14

Les Diablerets Switzerland
30.1.83

1	Quario	ITA	1:21.72
2	H Wenzel	LIE	1:22.29
3	D Tlalka	POL	1:22.50
4	Steiner	AUT	1:22.69
5	P Wenzel	LIE	1:22.72
6	McKinney	USA	1:22.86
7	Kronbichler	AUT	1:22.95
8	Zini	ITA	1:23.16
9	M Epple	BRD	1:23.24
10	Pelen	FRA	1:23.43
11	Magoni	ITA	1:23.80
12	M Tlalka	POL	1:24.29
13	Preuss	USA	1:24.32
14	Gerg	BRD	1:24.53
15	M Hess	SUI	1:24.73

Davos delight: Erika Hess, winner Tamara McKinney, Perrine Pelen

Maribor Yugoslavia
9.2.83

1	E Hess	SUI	1:42.68
2	H Wenzel	LIE	1:42.96
3	Kronbichler	AUT	1:43.10
4	P Wenzel	LIE	1:43.62
5	Zini	ITA	1:44.23
6	D Tlalka	POL	1:44.25
7	M Epple	BRD	1:44.45
8	Grabowska	POL	1:44.62
9	M Hess	SUI	1:44.93
10	Fernandez	SPA	1:45.43
11	Kinshofer	BRD	1:45.46
12	Nansoz	SUI	1:45.64
13	Oertli	SUI	1:46.00
14	Magoni	ITA	1:46.04
15	Serrat	FRA	1:46.06

Vysoke Tatry Czechoslovakia
12.2.83

1	Quario	ITA	1:33.40
2	E Hess	SUI	1:33.71
3	M Tlalka	POL	1:34.29
4	Steiner	AUT	1:34.38
5	Konzett	LIE	1:34.81
6	Zini	ITA	1:35.18
7	P Wenzel	LIE	1:35.52
8	D Tlalka	POL	1:37.02
9	Zavadlav	JUG	1:37.37
10	Charvatova	TCH	1:37.49
11	Magoni	ITA	1:37.80
12	Soelkner	AUT	1:37.83
13	Buder	AUT	1:37.87
14	Rey	FRA	1:38.15
15	Serrat	FRA	1:38.28

Waterville Valley USA
8.3.83

1	Steiner	AUT	1:33.84
2	McKinney	USA	1:34.21
3	H Wenzel	LIE	1:34.23
4	M Hess	SUI	1:34.53
5	M Tlalka	POL	1:34.63
6	Kronbichler	AUT	1:34.83
	Charvatova	TCH	1:34.83
8	Barbier	FRA	1:34.89
9	Zini	ITA	1:35.22
10	D Tlalka	POL	1:35.39
11	P Wenzel	LIE	1:35.72
12	Rey	FRA	1:35.80
13	Serrat	FRA	1:35.89
14	Quario	ITA	1:35.96
15	Gerg	BRD	1:36.24

Furano Japan
20.3.83

1	McKinney	USA	1:11.80
2	E Hess	SUI	1:12.00
3	M Tlalka	POL	1:12.12
4	H Wenzel	LIE	1:12.25
5	Konzett	LIE	1:12.94
6	Steiner	AUT	1:12.97
7	D Tlalka	POL	1:13.15
8	Magoni	ITA	1:13.36
9	Zini	ITA	1:13.60
10	Kronbichler	AUT	1:14.03
11	Charvatova	TCH	1:14.12
12	M Epple	BRD	1:14.28
13	Frigo	ITA	1:14.44
14	I Epple	BRD	1:14.51
15	Nelson	USA	1:15.15

WOMEN/SUPER AND GIANT SLALOM

1983

1	T McKinney	USA	120
2	C Nelson	USA	83
3	M Epple	BRD	81
4	E Hess	SUI	78
5	H Wenzel	LIE	77
6	F Serrat	FRA	68
7	I Epple	BRD	65
8	A F Rey	FRA	64
9	E Kirchler	AUT	46
10	M Walliser	SUI	40
11	Z Haas	SUI	38
12	C Cooper	USA	32
13	O Charvatova	TCH	30
14	C Merle	FRA	29
15	M Figini	SUI	25
16	P Pelen	FRA	24
	P Wenzel	LIE	24
18	M Gerg	BRD	23
19	A Kronbichler	AUT	22
20	H Barbier	FRA	20
	E Chaud	FRA	20
22	M Hess	SUI	18
23	C Riedl	BRD	15
24	U Konzett	LIE	13
25	D Zini	ITA	12
26	B Fernandez	SPA	9
	D Armstrong	USA	9
28	E Medzihradska	TCH	5
29	C Quittet	FRA	4
30	H Preuss	USA	3
31	H Wiesler	BRD	2
32	F Stevenin	ITA	1

Val d'Isère France
8.12.82

1	E Hess	SUI	2:22.12
2	McKinney	USA	2:22.87
3	H Wenzel	LIE	2:23.66
4	Kirchler	AUT	2:23.85
5	Barbier	FRA	2:23.94
6	Serrat	FRA	2:24.08
7	Konzett	LIE	2:24.14
8	M Epple	BRD	2:24.25
9	Cooper	USA	2:24.35
10	Rey	FRA	2:24.63
11	Medzihradska	TCH	2:25.50
	Zini	ITA	2:25.50
13	Pelen	FRA	2:25.79
14	Armstrong	USA	2:25.84
15	Fernandez	SPA	2:25.99

Verbier Switzerland
9.1.83 Super

1	I Epple	BRD	1:16.70
2	H Wenzel	LIE	1:16.94
3	McKinney	USA	1:16.96
4	Nelson	USA	1:17.31
5	Serrat	FRA	1:17.33
6	M Epple	BRD	1:17.48
7	Barbier	FRA	1:17.87
8	Chaud	FRA	1:17.89
9	Rey	FRA	1:18.04
10	Pelen	FRA	1:18.10
11	Kirchler	AUT	1:18.11
12	Konzett	LIE	1:18.32
	Haas	AUT	1:18.32
14	Kronbichler	AUT	1:18.34
15	Gerg	BRD	1:18.49

Verbier Switzerland
10.1.83 Super

1	Nelson	USA	1:08.56
2	Haas	AUT	1:09.16
3	I Epple	BRD	1:09.41
4	McKinney	USA	1:09.59
5	H Wenzel	LIE	1:09.69
6	M Epple	BRD	1:09.78
7	Chaud	FRA	1:10.16
8	Serrat	FRA	1:10.25
9	Kronbichler	AUT	1:10.41
10	Walliser	AUT	1:10.42
11	Cooper	USA	1:10.55
12	Quittet	FRA	1:10.64
13	Armstrong	USA	1:10.71
14	Zini	ITA	1:10.78
15	Rey	FRA	1:10.84

Megève/St Gervais France
23.1.83

1	McKinney	USA	2:29.60
2	Cooper	USA	2:30.62
3	Merle	FRA	2:30.96
4	Serrat	FRA	2:31.08
5	I Epple	BRD	2:31.12
6	E Hess	SUI	2:31.64
7	Rey	FRA	2:31.65
8	Haas	AUT	2:31.73
9	M Epple	BRD	2:31.94
10	Nelson	USA	2:32.07
11	H Wenzel	LIE	2:32.30
12	Zini	ITA	2:32.46
13	Preuss	USA	2:32.63
14	Gerg	BRD	2:32.81
15	Chaud	FRA	2:33.05

Mont Tremblant Canada
6.3.83

1	Rey	FRA	2:22.48
2	M Epple	BRD	2:22.57
3	E Hess	SUI	2:23.71
4	Kronbichler	AUT	2:23.72
5	P Wenzel	LIE	2:24.04
6	Charvatova	TCH	2:24.27
7	Walliser	SUI	2:24.32
8	Fernandez	SPA	2:24.40
9	Kirchler	AUT	2:24.41
10	Riedl	AUT	2:24.55
11	Nelson	USA	2:24.61
12	Figini	SUI	2:24.65
13	Merle	FRA	2:24.91
14	Serrat	FRA	2:25.22
15	Stevenin	ITA	2:25.64

Veteran's victory: Cindy Nelson (*centre*) wins the Verbier Super G from Zoe Haas (*left*) and Irene Epple

Waterville Valley USA
9.3.83

1	McKinney	USA	2:18.44
2	M Epple	BRD	2:19.15
3	Serrat	FRA	2:19.54
4	E Hess	SUI	2:19.66
5	Nelson	USA	2:20.57
6	M Hess	SUI	2:20.83
7	Riedl	AUT	2:21.02
8	I Epple	BRD	2:21.03
9	Gerg	BRD	2:21.09
10	H Wenzel	LIE	2:21.25
11	Kirchler	AUT	2:21.38
12	P Wenzel	LIE	2:21.85
13	Charvatova	TCH	2:22.00
14	Chaud	FRA	2:22.03
15	Walliser	SUI	2:22.35

Waterville Valley USA
10.3.83

1	McKinney	USA	2:18.72
2	M Epple	BRD	2:19.25
3	Nelson	USA	2:19.94
4	Figini	SUI	2:20.14
5	E Hess	SUI	2:20.17
	Rey	FRA	2:20.17
7	Walliser	SUI	2:20.74
8	M Hess	SUI	2:20.76
9	Gerg	BRD	2:20.88
10	I Epple	BRD	2:20.89
11	Kirchler	AUT	2:21.09
12	P Wenzel	LIE	2:21.10
13	Haas	AUT	2:21.12

14 Wiesler	BRD	2:21.74
15 Charvatova	TCH	2:21.82

Vail USA
12.3.83

1 McKinney	USA	2:23.43
2 Nelson	USA	2:24.05
3 E Hess	SUI	2:25.32
4 Rey	FRA	2:25.98
5 M Epple	BRD	2:26.02
6 Kirchler	AUT	2:26.40
7 Figini	SUI	2:26.57
8 Pelen	FRA	2:26.88
9 Charvatova	TCH	2:26.92
10 I Epple	BRD	2:27.18
11 P Wenzel	LIE	2:27.21
12 Armstrong	USA	2:27.39
13 H Wenzel	LIE	2:27.67
14 Gerg	BRD	2:27.98
15 Zini	ITA	2:28.07

America celebrates: Tamara McKinney pours champagne for former President Gerald Ford after winning Vail. Erika Hess is third

Furano Japan
18.3.83

1 H Wenzel	LIE	2:31.23
2 Serrat	FRA	2:33.18
3 Walliser	SUI	2:33.40
4 Kirchler	AUT	2:33.71
5 Merle	FRA	2:33.89
6 Nelson	USA	2:33.90
7 Charvatova	TCH	2:34.06
8 M Epple	BRD	2:34.39
9 Pelen	FRA	2:34.86
10 E Hess	SUI	2:34.87
11 Gerg	BRD	2:34.93
12 McKinney	USA	2:34.98
13 Haas	AUT	2:35.14
14 I Epple	BRD	2:35.30
15 Kronbichler	AUT	2:35.42

WOMEN/COMBINED

Val d'Isère

1 Kirchler	AUT
2 McKinney	USA
3 E Hess	SUI
4 H Wenzel	LIE
5 Walliser	SUI
6 I Epple	BRD
7 Graham	CAN
8 Ganterova-Soltysova	TCH
9 Nelson	USA
10 Charvatova	TCH
11 Armstrong	USA
12 Wiesler	BRD
13 Cooper	USA
14 Bozon	FRA
15 de Agostini	SUI

Sansicario/Piancavallo

1 Cooper	USA
2 E Hess	SUI
3 H Wenzel	LIE
4 Kronbichler	AUT
5 Wiesler	BRD
6 Oertli	SUI
7 Gutensohn	AUT
8 I Epple	BRD
9 Kirchler	AUT
10 Valesova	TCH
11 Armstrong	USA
12 Robin	SUI
13 Twardokens	USA
14 Stotz	BRD
15 D Tlalka	POL

Schruns/Tschagguns

1 Charvatova	TCH
2 Eder	AUT
3 Serrat	FRA
4 Oertli	SUI
5 I Epple	BRD
6 Nelson	USA
7 Gutensohn	AUT
8 Haas	AUT
9 Wiesler	BRD
10 Figini	SUI
11 Kiehl	BRD
12 Medzihradska	TCH
13 Difant	FRA

Les Diablerets

1 H Wenzel	LIE
2 Gerg	BRD
3 Kirchler	AUT
4 Nelson	USA
5 I Epple	BRD
6 McKinney	USA
7 Eder	AUT
8 Haas	AUT
9 Stotz	BRD
10 Figini	SUI
11 Valesova	TCH
12 Wiesler	BRD
13 D Tlalka	POL
14 Twardokens	USA
15 Grabowska	POL

WORLD CUP CALENDAR 1983-1984

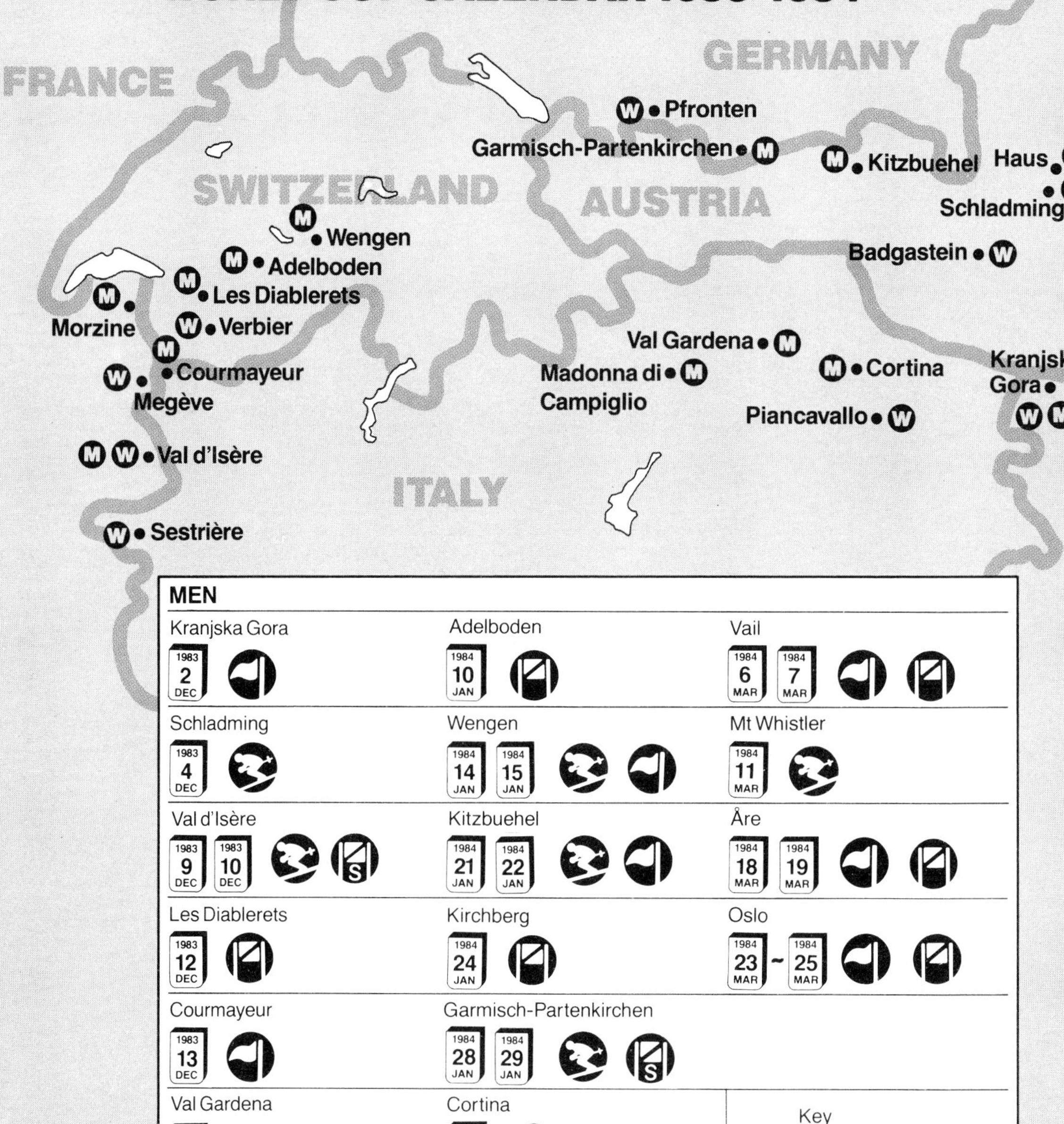

MEN

Venue	Date(s)	Events
Kranjska Gora	2 DEC 1983	Special slalom
Schladming	4 DEC 1983	Downhill
Val d'Isère	9 DEC 1983, 10 DEC 1983	Downhill, Super giant slalom
Les Diablerets	12 DEC 1983	Giant slalom
Courmayeur	13 DEC 1983	Special slalom
Val Gardena	18 DEC 1983	Downhill
Madonna di Campiglio	20 DEC 1983, 21 DEC 1983	Special slalom, Super giant slalom
Morzine	6 JAN 1984, 7 JAN 1984	Downhill, Special slalom
Adelboden	10 JAN 1984	Giant slalom
Wengen	14 JAN 1984, 15 JAN 1984	Downhill, Special slalom
Kitzbuehel	21 JAN 1984, 22 JAN 1984	Downhill, Special slalom
Kirchberg	24 JAN 1984	Giant slalom
Garmisch-Partenkirchen	28 JAN 1984, 29 JAN 1984	Downhill, Super giant slalom
Cortina	2 FEB 1984	Downhill
Borovetz	4 FEB 1984, 5 FEB 1984	Special slalom, Giant slalom
Aspen	3 MAR 1984, 4 MAR 1984	Downhill, Giant slalom
Vail	6 MAR 1984, 7 MAR 1984	Special slalom, Giant slalom
Mt Whistler	11 MAR 1984	Downhill
Åre	18 MAR 1984, 19 MAR 1984	Special slalom, Giant slalom
Oslo	23 MAR 1984 ~ 25 MAR 1984	Special slalom, Giant slalom

Key

- Downhill
- Special slalom
- Giant slalom
- Super giant slalom

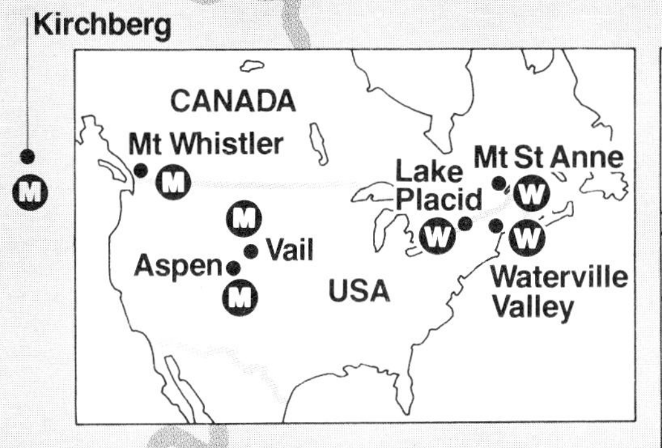

Maribor

YUGOSLAVIA

W Women's events

M Men's events

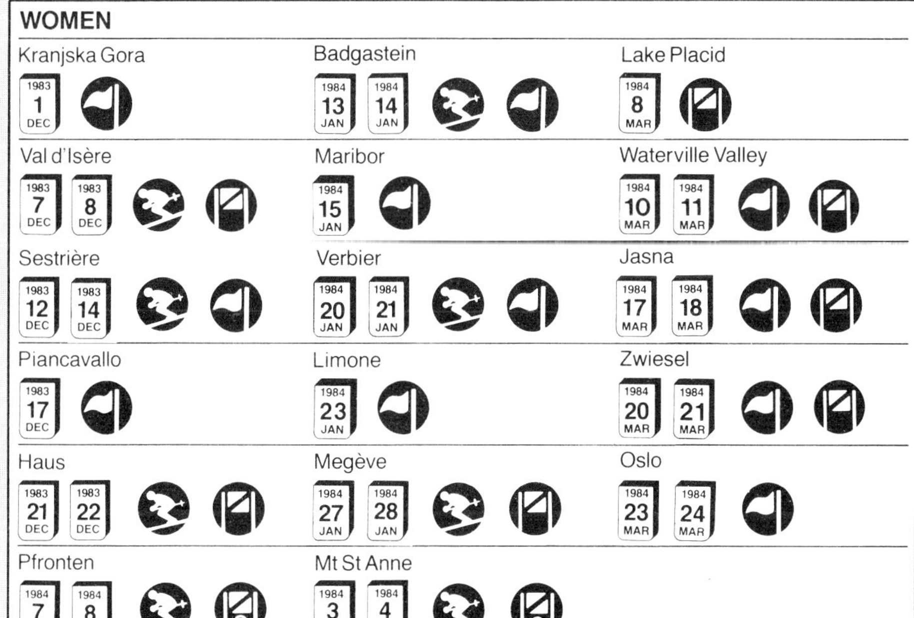

WOMEN

Kranjska Gora	1983 1 DEC
Badgastein	1984 13 JAN, 1984 14 JAN
Lake Placid	1984 8 MAR
Val d'Isère	1983 7 DEC, 1983 8 DEC
Maribor	1984 15 JAN
Waterville Valley	1984 10 MAR, 1984 11 MAR
Sestrière	1983 12 DEC, 1983 14 DEC
Verbier	1984 20 JAN, 1984 21 JAN
Jasna	1984 17 MAR, 1984 18 MAR
Piancavallo	1983 17 DEC
Limone	1984 23 JAN
Zwiesel	1984 20 MAR, 1984 21 MAR
Haus	1983 21 DEC, 1983 22 DEC
Megève	1984 27 JAN, 1984 28 JAN
Oslo	1984 23 MAR, 1984 24 MAR
Pfronten	1984 7 JAN, 1984 8 JAN
Mt St Anne	1984 3 MAR, 1984 4 MAR

WORLD CUP COMBINED EVENTS

Men

1 Val d'Isère	Downhill – Super slalom
2 Madonna di Campiglio	Special slalom – Super slalom
3 Wengen	Downhill – Special slalom
4 Kitzbuehel	Downhill – Special slalom
5 Garmisch-Partenkirchen	Downhill – Super slalom

Women

1 Val d'Isère	Downhill – Giant slalom
2 Sestrière	Downhill – Special slalom
3 Bad Gastein	Downhill – Special slalom
4 Verbier	Downhill – Special slalom
5 Megève	Downhill – Giant slalom

OLYMPIC GAMES 1936–80

Alpine skiing events were included in the Winter Olympic Games for the first time in 1936, but medals were only awarded for the Combined. In 1948 medals were given for Downhill, Slalom and Combined. In 1952 the Giant Slalom was added but medals were no longer awarded for the Combined. Ski Jumping has been part of the Winter Olympics since 1924. The 90-metre hill was added in 1964.

MEN

1936 Garmisch-Partenkirchen, GER

Downhill
1 B Ruud NOR
2 F Pfnür GER
3 G Lantschner GER

Slalom
1 F Pfnür GER
2 G Lantschner GER
3 E Allais FRA

Combined
1 F Pfnür GER
2 G Lantschner GER
3 E Allais FRA

70-m Jump
1 B Ruud NOR
2 S Eriksson SWE
3 R Andersen NOR

1948 St Moritz, SUI

Downhill
1 H Oreiller FRA
2 F Gabl AUT
3 K Molitor SUI
R Olinger SUI

Slalom
1 E Reinalter SUI
2 J Couttet FRA
3 H Oreiller FRA

Combined
1 H Oreiller FRA
2 K Molitor SUI
3 J Couttet FRA

70-m Jump
1 P Hugstedt NOR
2 B Ruud NOR
3 T Schjelderup NOR

1952 Oslo, NOR

Downhill
1 Z Colo ITA
2 O Schneider AUT
3 C Pravda AUT

Slalom
1 O Schneider AUT
2 S Eriksen NOR
3 G Berge NOR

Giant Slalom
1 S Eriksen NOR
2 C Pravda AUT
3 T Spiess AUT

70-m Jump
1 A Bergmann NOR
2 T Falkanger NOR
3 K Holmström SWE

1956 Cortina d'Ampezzo, ITA

Downhill
1 A Sailer AUT
2 R Fellay SUI
3 A Molterer AUT

Slalom
1 A Sailer AUT
2 C Igaya JPN
3 S Sollander SWE

Giant Slalom
1 A Sailer AUT
2 A Molterer AUT
3 W Schuster AUT

Combined
1 A Sailer AUT
2 C Bozon FRA
3 S Sollander SWE

70-m Jump
1 A Hyvärinen FIN
2 A Kallakorpi FIN
3 H Glass GER

1960 Squaw Valley, USA

Downhill

1	J Vuarnet	FRA
2	H-P Lanig	GER
3	G Perillat	FRA

Slalom

1	E Hinterseer	AUT
2	M Leitner	AUT
3	C Bozon	FRA

Giant Slalom

1	R Staub	SUI
2	J Stiegler	AUT
3	E Hinterseer	AUT

Combined

1	G Perillat	FRA
2	C Bozon	FRA
3	H-P Lanig	GER

70-m Jump

1	H Recknagel	GER
2	N Halonen	FIN
3	O Leodolter	AUT

Toni Sailer

Jean-Claude Killy

Gustavo Thoeni

1964 Innsbruck, AUT

Downhill

1	E Zimmerman	AUT
2	L Lacroix	FRA
3	W Bartels	GER

Slalom

1	J Stiegler	AUT
2	W Kidd	USA
3	J Huega	USA

Giant Slalom

1	F Bonlieu	FRA
2	K Schranz	AUT
3	J Stiegler	AUT

Combined

1	L Leitner	GER
2	G Nenning	AUT
3	W Kidd	USA

70-m Jump

1	V Kankkonen	FIN
2	T Engan	NOR
3	T Brandtzaeg	NOR

90-m Jump

1	T Engan	NOR
2	V Kankkonen	FIN
3	T Brandtzaeg	NOR

1968 Grenoble, FRA

Downhill

1	J-C Killy	FRA
2	G Perillat	FRA
3	J-D Daetwyler	SUI

Slalom

1	J-C Killy	FRA
2	H Huber	AUT
3	A Matt	AUT

Giant Slalom

1	J-C Killy	FRA
2	W Favre	SUI
3	H Messner	AUT

Combined

1	J-C Killy	FRA
2	D Giovanoli	SUI
3	H Messner	AUT

70-m Jump

1	J Raska	TCH
2	R Bachler	AUT
3	B Preiml	AUT

90-m Jump

1	V Belussov	SOV
2	J Raska	TCH
3	L Grini	NOR

1972 Sapporo, JPN

Downhill

1	B Russi	SUI
2	R Collombin	FRA
3	H Messner	AUT

Slalom

1	F Ochoa	SPA
2	G Thoeni	ITA
3	R Thoeni	ITA

Giant Slalom

1	G Thoeni	ITA
2	E Bruggmann	SUI
3	W Mattle	SUI

Combined

1	G Thoeni	ITA
2	W Tresch	SUI
3	J Hunter	CAN

70-m Jump

1	Y Kasaya	JPN
2	A Konno	JPN
3	S Aochi	JPN

90-m Jump

1	W Fortuna	POL
2	W Steiner	SUI
3	R Schmidt	DDR

Champion chat: Franz Klammer and Bernhard Russi, 1976 and 1972 Olympic downhill winners

Karl Schranz: denied at Grenoble, expelled at Sapporo

1976 Innsbruck, AUT

Downhill		Slalom		Giant Slalom	
1 F Klammer	AUT	1 P Gros	ITA	1 H Hemmi	SUI
2 B Russi	SUI	2 G Thoeni	ITA	2 E Good	SUI
3 H Plank	ITA	3 W Frommelt	LIE	3 I Stenmark	SWE

Combined		70-m Jump		90-m Jump	
1 G Thoeni	ITA	1 H-G Aschenbach	DDR	1 K Schnabl	AUT
2 W Frommelt	LIE	2 J Danneberg	DDR	2 A Innauer	AUT
3 G Jones	USA	3 K Schnabl	AUT	3 G Glass	DDR

1980 Lake Placid, USA

Downhill		Slalom		Giant Slalom	
1 L Stock	AUT	1 I Stenmark	SWE	1 I Stenmark	SWE
2 P Wirnsberger	AUT	2 B Krizaj	JUG	2 A Wenzel	LIE
3 S Podborski	CAN	3 B Fjaellberg	SWE	3 H Enn	AUT

Combined		70-m Jump		90-m Jump	
1 P Mahre	USA	1 A Innauer	AUT	1 J Tormanen	FIN
2 A Wenzel	LIE	2 M Deckert	DDR	2 H Neuper	AUT
3 L Stock	AUT	3 H Yagi	JPN	3 J Puikkonen	FIN

WOMEN

1936 Garmisch-Partenkirchen, GER

Downhill		Slalom		Combined	
1 L Schou-Nilsen	NOR	1 C Cranz	GER	1 C Cranz	GER
2 L Resch	GER	2 K Grasegger	GER	2 K Grasegger	GER
3 K Grasegger	GER	3 E Steuri	SUI	3 L Schou-Nilsen	NOR

1948 St Moritz, SUI

Downhill		Slalom		Combined	
1 H Schlunegger	SUI	1 G Fraser	USA	1 T Beiser	AUT
2 T Beiser	AUT	2 A Meyer	SUI	2 G Fraser	USA
3 R Hammerer	AUT	3 E Mahringer	AUT	3 E Mahringer	AUT

1952 Oslo, NOR

Downhill		Slalom		Giant Slalom	
1 T Beiser-Jochum	AUT	1 A Mead-Lawrence	USA	1 A Mead-Lawrence	USA
2 A Buchner	GER	2 O Reichert	GER	2 D Rom	AUT
3 G Minuzzo	ITA	3 A Buchner	GER	3 A Buchner	GER

1956 Cortina d'Ampezzo, ITA

Downhill		Slalom		Giant Slalom	
1 M Berthod	SUI	1 R Colliard	SUI	1 O Reichert	GER
2 F Daenzer	SUI	2 R Schoepf	AUT	2 J Frandl	AUT
3 L Wheeler	CAN	3 E Sidorova	SOV	3 D Hochleitner	AUT

Combined	
1 M Berthod	SUI
2 F Daenzer	SUI
3 G Chenal-Minuzzo	ITA

1960 Squaw Valley, USA

Downhill		Slalom		Giant Slalom	
1 H Biebl	GER	1 A Heggtveit	CAN	1 Y Ruegg	SUI
2 P Pitou	USA	2 B Snite	USA	2 P Pitou	USA
3 T Hecher	AUT	3 B Henneberger	GER	3 C Chenal-Minuzzo	ITA

Combined	
1 A Heggtveit	CAN
2 S Sperl	GER
3 B Henneberger	GER

1964 Innsbruck, AUT

Downhill		Slalom		Giant Slalom	
1 C Haas	AUT	1 C Goitschel	FRA	1 M Goitschel	FRA
2 E Zimmermann	AUT	2 M Goitschel	FRA	2 C Goitschel	FRA
3 T Hecher	AUT	3 J Saubert	USA	J Saubert	USA

Combined	
1 M Goitschel	FRA
2 C Haas	AUT
3 E Zimmermann	AUT

1968 Grenoble, FRA

Downhill		Slalom		Giant Slalom	
1 O Pall	AUT	1 M Goitschel	FRA	1 N Greene	CAN
2 I Mir	FRA	2 N Greene	CAN	2 A Famose	FRA
3 C Haas	AUT	3 A Famose	FRA	3 F Bochatay	SUI

Combined	
1 N Greene	CAN
2 M Goitschel	FRA
3 A Famose	FRA

Master class: Hanni Wenzel (*left*), Marie-Therese Nadig and Annemarie Moser-Proell

Rosi Mittermaier

1972 Sapporo, JPN

Downhill

1	M-T Nadig	SUI
2	A Proell	AUT
3	S Corrock	USA

Slalom

1	B Cochran	USA
2	D Debernard	FRA
3	F Steurer	FRA

Giant Slalom

1	M-T Nadig	SUI
2	A Proell	AUT
3	W Drexel	AUT

Combined

1	A Proell	AUT
2	F Steurer	FRA
3	T Förland	NOR

1976 Innsbruck, AUT

Downhill

1	R Mittermaier	BRD
2	B Totschnigg	AUT
3	C Nelson	USA

Slalom

1	R Mittermaier	BRD
2	C Giordani	ITA
3	H Wenzel	LIE

Giant Slalom

1	K Kreiner	AUT
2	R Mittermaier	BRD
3	D Debernard	FRA

Combined

1	R Mittermaier	BRD
2	D Debernard	FRA
3	H Wenzel	LIE

1980 Lake Placid, USA

Downhill

1	A Moser-Proell	AUT
2	H Wenzel	LIE
3	M T Nadig	SUI

Slalom

1	H Wenzel	LIE
2	C Kinshofer	BRD
3	E Hess	SUI

Giant Slalom

1	H Wenzel	LIE
2	I Epple	BRD
3	P Pelen	FRA

Combined

1	H Wenzel	LIE
2	C Nelson	USA
3	I Eberle	AUT